Masterpiece

ICONIC Houses

Masterpiece
ICONIC Houses

BY GREAT CONTEMPORARY ARCHITECTS

Edited by Beth Browne

images
Publishing

Published in Australia in 2012 by
The Images Publishing Group Pty Ltd
ABN 89 059 734 431
6 Bastow Place, Mulgrave, Victoria 3170, Australia
Tel: +61 3 9561 5544 Fax: +61 3 9561 4860
books@imagespublishing.com
www.imagespublishing.com

National Library of Australia Cataloguing-in-Publication entry

Title: Masterpiece : iconic houses by great
contemporary architects / edited by Beth Browne.

ISBN: 9781864704532 (hbk.)

Subjects: Architect-designed houses – History – 20th century
                 – Pictorial works.
                 Architect-designed houses – History – 21st century
                 – Pictorial works.
                 Architect-designed houses – Designs and plans.

Dewey Number: 728.370904

Production by The Graphic Image Studio Pty Ltd, Mulgrave,
Australia
www.tgis.com.au

Pre-publishing services by United Graphic Pte Ltd, Singapore

Printed by 1010 Printing International Limited in China on 140 gsm
Gold East Matt Art paper

IMAGES has included on its website a page for special notices
in relation to this and its other publications. Please visit
www.imagespublishing.com.

CONTENTS

5°35' at Craignish

Argyll, United Kingdom

CAMERON WEBSTER ARCHITECTS

Located in the grounds of Craignish Castle, next to a rocky outcrop surrounded by sycamore and beech trees, this house won a Saltire Housing Award in 2011.

Planning conditions stipulated that the house should be rendered with a pitched slate roof; however, the client wanted a modern house for his wife (an artist and accomplished cook) and himself (a technologically savvy retired helicopter pilot and expert plantsman). The planners were sympathetic to this, as the house could not be seen from the castle, and the flat roof allowed it to be largely hidden behind the rocky outcrop.

The building is tucked into the outcrop, with the main living areas and master bedroom linked by an enfilade running along the southwest elevation, offering a commanding view to Loch Beag. The roof steps up to reflect the site contours

1 Roof profile steps up following the site contours

9

and to provide a generous and sunny volume to the large kitchen that forms the heart of the house. Glazed doors allow access from the kitchen and living room directly onto the top of the outcrop.

The master bedroom is cantilevered over the front door, providing a sheltered entrance area and carport. The two guest bedrooms, cloakrooms and service accommodation are on the first floor, with eastern views to a small pond and garden. The staircase leads to the public rooms above, and is matched externally by steps in the rock, further linking the interior to the external environment.

The structure is a steel frame, with heavily insulated walls clad in zinc. The floors are tiled throughout, with oak joinery and full-height glazing on the south and west elevations to take advantage of solar gain. Although a gas boiler proved the most economical solution for heating, the walls are highly insulated with cellulose insulation, while underfloor heating and a full mechanical heat-recovery system are integrated into the building, making the energy demand very low, even in mid winter. A wood-burning stove is located in the living area and there is provision for solar collectors for hot water.

5

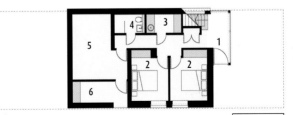

6

1	Entrance hall
2	Bedroom
3	Utility room
4	Shower room
5	Plant/store
6	Bins/store
7	Dining/living area
8	Kitchen
9	Pantry
10	Open living/library
11	Bathroom
12	Study/bedroom
13	Master bedroom
14	Ensuite
15	Dressing room

0   4m

2   View of house from garden

3   House in the snow, sitting over the rocky outcrop

4   Evening view of house against rocky landscape

5   Second floor plan

6   First floor plan

7 Internal and external stairs sit side by side against the rock

8 Main living area sitting over rock towards views of the loch

9 Sunny enfilade linking main spaces with views to the loch

10 Places to sit along enfilade utilise the space, light and views to the best advantage

PHOTOGRAPHY: KEITH HUNTER PHOTOGRAPHY

BERBERIAN Residence

Los Angeles, California, United States | **LANDRY DESIGN GROUP**

The primary concept for this residence was to design a home that incorporates modernist philosophies while being well adapted to today's contemporary lifestyle. Located in a prestigious residential community on a 2-hectare (4-acre) site, the house was further enhanced by incorporating the site's large mature trees into the design. The prominence of these existing trees was such that they actually dictated the orientation and layout of the home, resulting in a project that becomes an integral part of the landscape from both an exterior and interior point of view.

The exterior of the home comprises large glass walls, smooth hand-trowelled stucco and Pennsylvania bluestone laid in a ledger pattern. All of these materials were chosen for their ability to relate to each other as well as for their compatibility with the colours and textures of the natural surroundings.

1 Exterior view towards entry court

15

Within the home are bright, open spaces with generous openings to the exterior landscape – offering dramatic backdrops for the owner's sculpture collection. Strategically placed throughout the interior of the home are continued elements of the stone used on the exterior of the building. This textured surface flows through the interior spaces in opposition to the extensive glazing. The expanses of glass provide views of the statuesque trees sitting in the landscape, extending the interior feel of the home, while the stone walls purposefully limit views to the open interior spaces. Together these elements establish a strong dialogue between architecture and landscape, between interior and exterior, and between solid and void.

2   Rear view

3   Exterior view of rear from pool

4   View of two-storey foyer curtain wall and main stair

5   View towards living room and second-floor gallery from main stair

6   Second floor plan

7   First floor plan

1 Balcony
2 Master bedroom
3 Master bathroom
4 Closet
5 Master closet
6 Gym
7 Guest bedroom
8 Storage
9 Bedroom
10 Skylight
11 Gallery
12 Open to below
13 Laundry

6

1 Covered entry
2 Foyer/main stair
3 Powder room
4 Library
5 Covered loggia
6 Living room
7 Family room
8 Breakfast room
9 Kitchen
10 Playroom
11 Gallery
12 Study
13 Maid's bedroom
14 Garage
15 Laundry
16 Dining room
17 Entry court

0   50ft

7

PHOTOGRAPHY: ERHARD PFEIFFER

11

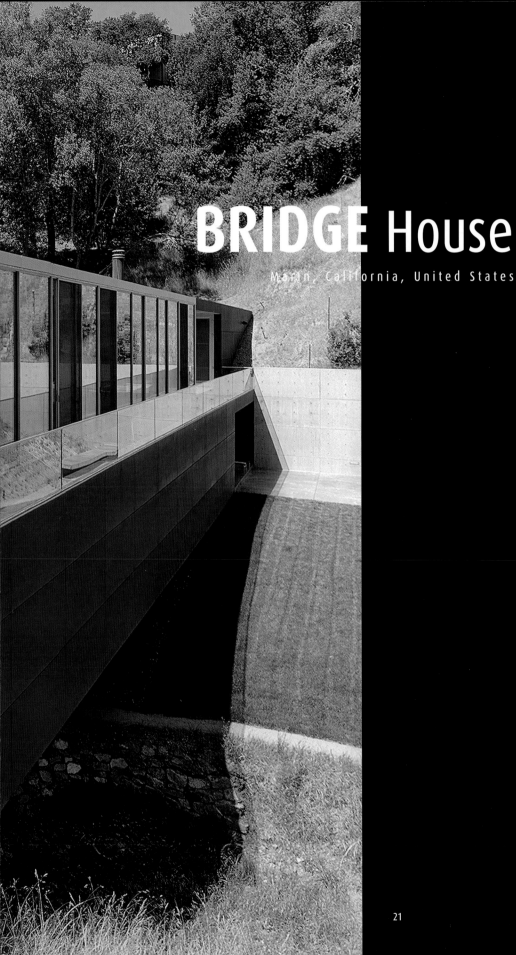

BRIDGE House

Marin, California, United States

STANLEY SAITOWITZ | NATOMA ARCHITECTS INC.

The Bridge House is sited on 15 acres of wooded grasslands with a ravine running through. The house bridges the ravine, spanning east to west.

The house is a continuous 7-metre-wide (22-foot) two-storey bar. A stair leads up to the entry court. The living areas, located on the upper level, feature continuous glass walls that face north towards the hill. The bedrooms below also feature continuous floor-to-ceiling glazing, though facing south towards the theatre in the landscape.

From above and below two contrasting experiences of the site are realised – one broad and expansive, the other defined and closed.

Along the upper bridge are two open courts: one for the entry, the other connecting the main house to the pool and guesthouse. A deck links these courts on the north side, and connects to paths that lead into the landscape up the hill.

1   North side of bridge

The walls and roof are clad in Corten steel plate; viewed from above, the rusty bar bridges the golden, grassy slopes. A blue pool branches off the bar and projects from the hill.

2   Driveway view

3   Entry court

4   South side of bridge

5   Entry

PHOTOGRAPHY: RIEN VAN RIJTHOVEN

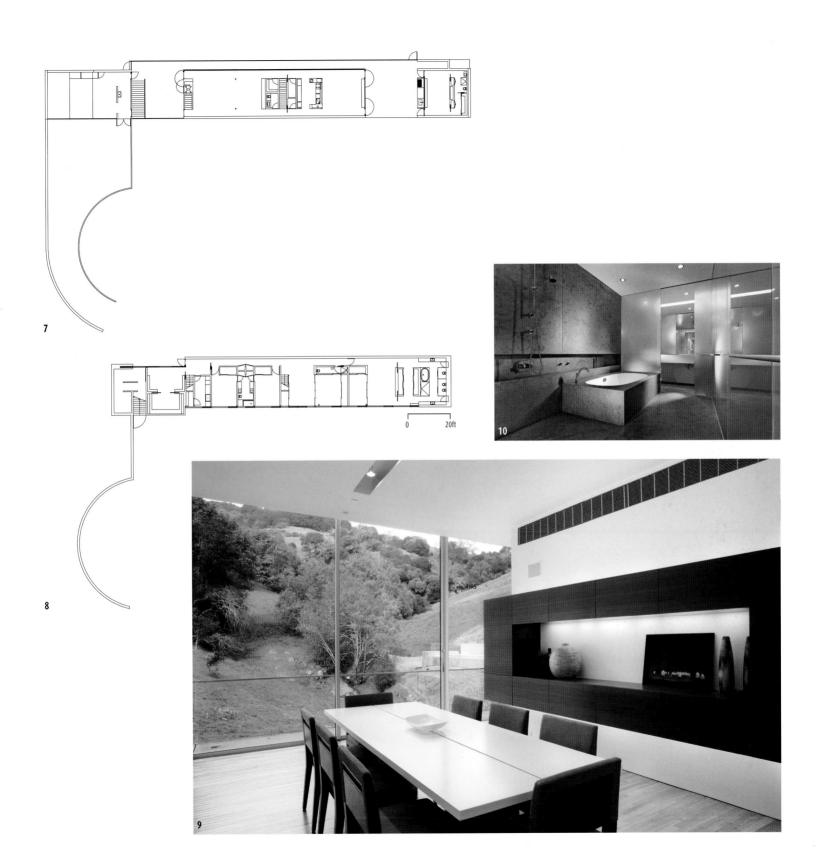

7

8

0   20ft

10

9

BRUSSELS House

Brussels, Belgium

PHILIPPE SAMYN AND PARTNERS

This 600-square-metre (6500-square-foot) house for an artist incorporates the street level of an existing small house, which now accommodates the entry hall, family room and kitchen; while the living room and stairway are located in the extension to the building.

The second floor includes the master bedroom and master bathroom, as well as five children's rooms with ensuites. A mezzanine, protected by textile netting, leads to the glass-wall façade.

The house is contained by curved and planted façades that are closed to the neighbours to the north, east and south for privacy. In contrast, the west façade is constructed entirely with glass, as if it were one huge partitioned window.

Translucent white polyester curtains, 1.6 metres (5 feet) in width, are suspended from the top of the structure to the first floor, running along this great window to ensure shade in the summer months.

1   The west façade constructed entirely of glass

2   The lush vertical garden façade features a mix of exotic plants

3   Wood-clad interior featuring built-in display cases

4   A sliver of glazing runs from the floor into the ceiling, providing additional daylighting

5   Geometric forms create artistic aspects within

6   Third floor plan

7   Second floor plan

8   The custom timber stair

9   First floor plan

PHOTOGRAPHY: © MARIE-FRANÇOISE PLISSART; PHILIPPE SAMYN AND PARTNERS, ARCHITECTS & ENGINEERS

Initially conceived as a wall of ivy with a patinated copper roof, the vertical-garden façade now comprises a selection of exotic plants chosen by the botanical artist Patrick Blanc, and extends to cover the roof. The structure, insulation and water-tightness of the envelope were planned accordingly, and building physics issues resolved in order to provide the necessary support systems, irrigation and fertilisation systems for the plants, which are set into a felt support stapled to rigid PVC panels.

5

8

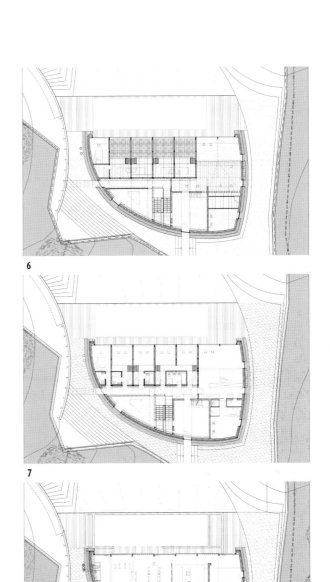

6

7

9

0   5m

1

CARRILLO Residence

Pacific Palisades, California, United States | **EHRLICH ARCHITECTS**

The Carrillo Residence occupies a long narrow site on the rim of Santa Monica Canyon with distant views of the Pacific Ocean. Designed for a young couple with two children, the house addresses the formal and informal needs of the family while taking advantage of the Southern California climate and views. The orientation of the house reinforces the geometry of the site. A series of stone masses defines the ground floor programme, while a pristine floating white box houses the bedroom wings and slides over and past the stone towards the canyon and the views.

The glass living room volume sits at the far end of the site next to the main bar of the house and divides the outdoor space into two distinct courts. The informal front court provides a protected sun-filled play yard for the children adjacent to the family zone. The formal rear court comprises an outdoor dining area, barbecue and infinity-edge pool and expands toward the view beyond. The living room

1   **View of the house from the entry gate: a meandering approach cuts across the 'family' courtyard inhabited by Lalanne sheep sculptures**

2

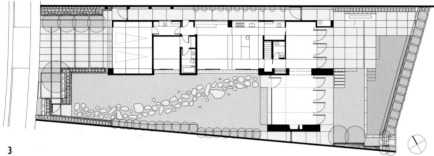

3

4

and dining room can be completely opened up to this court by a series of oversized pivot doors. The large expanses of glass in the living room visually connect the formal and informal domains and allow for the view to extend to the canyon beyond. The custom wood ceiling and custom-stained concrete inside and out emphasise this sense of visual continuity.

Internally, the formal adult zone and informal family zones (and the master suite and children's rooms above) are separated by the stair core and play area, and can be closed off from each other with pocket doors. Built-in cabinets are used throughout the home to divide larger spaces into smaller areas. The play area upstairs can be converted into a third bedroom if needed.

The cantilevered master bedroom creates a covered outdoor dining area and hovers out toward the canyon views. The angle of the roof above the bedroom terrace and the infinity edge of the pool are parallel to the geometry of the site and the canyon below.

2   Second floor plan

3   First floor plan

4   Floor-to-ceiling pivoting glass doors open to the back courtyard

5   The formal living area opens up to both the front and back courtyards creating an airy pavilion

6   View of family room and kitchen from the 'family' courtyard

7 Glass walls and pivot doors are anchored by solid travertine walls connecting the indoor and outdoor spaces

8 A freestanding walnut cabinet unit separates the kitchen and family living area

9 Designed as a separate space, the pavilion has a custom walnut ceiling, which visually sets the room apart from the rest of the house

10 Sliding glass doors allow the master suite to open up to panoramic views of the surrounding canyon and Pacific Ocean

11 Subtle colours and textures, including river-rock-tile flooring, create a retreat feel within the master bathroom

12 The open-plan kitchen features white laminate and walnut cabinetry

PHOTOGRAPHY: BARRY SCHWARTZ

DRUMLIN Hall

Dutchess County, New York, United States

PETER PENNOYER ARCHITECTS

Drumlin Hall, a 700-square-metre (7,500-square-foot) new classical stone house in Dutchess County, New York, is a modern-day version of a Federal-style villa – a house that revels in perfect proportion, rigorous geometry and the great flexibility of the classical idiom.

The exterior, faced in warm buff sandstone, is a lesson in symmetry and bows to the wealth of Regency houses designed by such architects as Henry Holland, Benjamin Latrobe, Sir John Soane and S. P. Cockerell. Each of the four principal façades has its own distinct personality.

The plan revolves around two central axes and succinctly absorbs all of the requisite rooms into a contained rectangle, with windows expressed symmetrically on the façades. In the stair hall, Greek Revival-inspired door casings, pilasters and standing door pediments carved

1   The north elevation is heroic in scale, with severe wings
     contrasting with the columned bay of the breakfast room
     and a massive chimney rising up through the roofs

with anthemia mark the entryways set along the long axis, while a set of faux-marble columns frames the library.

The drawing room was designed around an Italian mantle from the 1820s elaborately carved with vestal virgins and Mercury. The firm evoked the work of Minard Lafever in the design for the door casings and Aeolic pilasters, and wove in details such as a repeated star motif, which purposefully hints to the client's Texan heritage, to personalise the design. Painted wood floors were incorporated in the stair halls, bar and library as references to other important historic houses in the area, such as Edgewater.

In carrying out the great curving stair, the firm looked to Cheekwood, the Cheek estate in Nashville, Tennessee – a house the client admired. The composition and scale of the antique balustrade adorning Cheekwood's sweeping central stair was refined to fit the proportions of Drumlin Hall and metalworker Jean Wiart was commissioned to execute the delicately wrought pattern of garlands, pine cones and eagles. In the upstairs stair hall, the most dramatic interior in the house, the firm incorporated niches for sculpture – as it did in the stair – fusing art with architecture.

2   The name of the house was inspired by its setting in a valley of miniature hills, or drumlins, that were formed by glacial deposits

3   The east-facing portico opens off the living room and out onto the rolling fields of eastern Dutchess County

4   The pedimented south façade commands the long approach from the south and is marked by the tall terrace doors of the central rooms, carved panels and massive chimney stacks

5   Bas-relief cornucopias enrich the lunettes above the French doors on the pedimented south façade

6   Floor plan

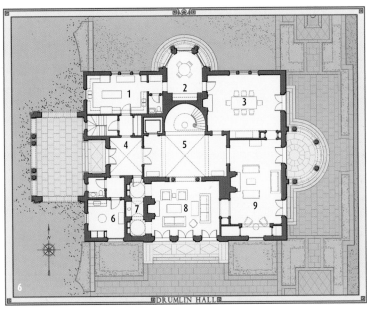

1 Kitchen
2 Breakfast room
3 Dining room
4 Entry hall
5 Stair hall
6 Gun room
7 Bar
8 Library
9 Drawing room

7   Every space within the house was designed to relate to the groin vault on the first floor and the dome on the second floor that mark the centre of the building

8   Two domed book recesses in the faux-bois panelled library connect to the bar concealed behind the chimney breast

9   Gold-leaf bead mouldings articulate the vaults in the bar

10 The large open space of the vaulted second-floor gallery is lit by a lay light at the centre of a handkerchief dome

11 The drawing room is the most heavily ornamented room in the house, with Greek Revival door casings and Aeolic pilasters inspired by the work of Minard Lafever

12 An antique balustrade at Cheekwood, the Cheek estate in Nashville, Tennessee, served as inspiration for the embellishment of Drumlin Hall's sweeping stair

PHOTOGRAPHY: JONATHAN WALLEN

1

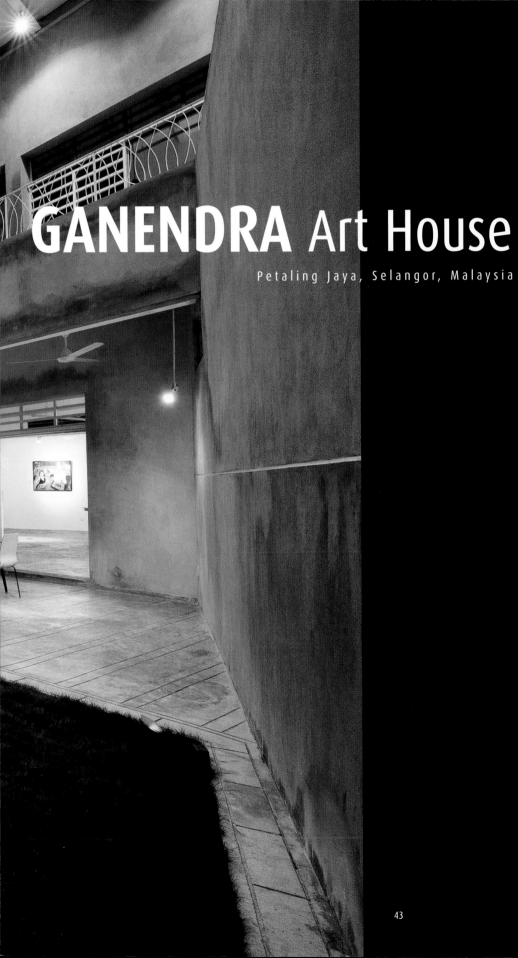

GANENDRA Art House

Petaling Jaya, Selangor, Malaysia | **KEN YEANG**

The client's brief was for a building that spoke to their commitment to good design, innovation, green principles and value. The house is designed to accommodate a range of uses – cultural and residential – and includes an experimental design element wherein cooling is provided by a downdraft vertical shaft (coined as a 'wind chimney'). It is targeted to meet Silver GBI rating.

The two-storey 630-square-metre (6800-square-foot) building requires little maintenance and will age gracefully due to features such as raw exterior finishes with creepers growing upwards to create pattern and texture. The building's public spaces will be used for exhibitions, lectures and social purposes. Benefitting from natural daylight and a high ceiling volume, these areas feature large, blank wall spaces for hanging artwork. Other functional spaces include an office and study room, an artist's studio, rooms for art

1   Courtyard at dusk

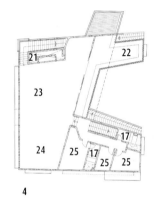

3

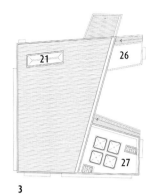

4

storage, a small open kitchen and wet kitchen, a utility room, a clothes-drying area, bathrooms and bedrooms. The semi-outdoor patio with built-in bar opens onto a courtyard, which serves as a backdrop for installation art. There is a segmented area outside for sculpture and the front garden can double as a parking area.

The building's configuration and orientation are based on the location's solar path. The front and back of the house are aligned, while the west (hot) side faces the noisy main road. Meeting the clients' requirements for organic interaction between the various spaces, the generally open layout and landscaped courtyard face east. The central courtyard, external patios and study room enjoy morning sun, while the bedrooms and bathrooms face south. The west side has minimum window openings to reduce solar heat gain and exposure to ambient road noise, with a double brick wall for greater cooling and noise insulation. Supported by a single column, the feature entrance canopy at the front driveway marks the entrance to the building and provides a wider frontage to the driveway.

2   Entrance view
3   Roof plan
4   Second floor plan
5   First floor plan

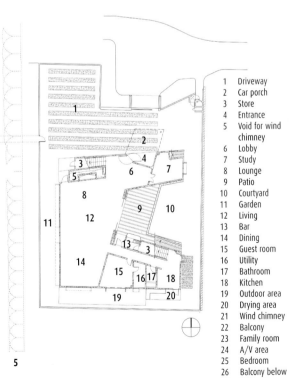

5

1	Driveway
2	Car porch
3	Store
4	Entrance
5	Void for wind chimney
6	Lobby
7	Study
8	Lounge
9	Patio
10	Courtyard
11	Garden
12	Living
13	Bar
14	Dining
15	Guest room
16	Utility
17	Bathroom
18	Kitchen
19	Outdoor area
20	Drying area
21	Wind chimney
22	Balcony
23	Family room
24	A/V area
25	Bedroom
26	Balcony below
27	Water storage

PHOTOGRAPHY: SGFA/SK CHONG, WWW.SHALINIGANENDRA.COM

1

THE HEN House

Fiscavaig, Isle of Skye, United Kingdom | **RURAL DESIGN**

This small holiday house is located in the township of Fiscavaig, on the western side of the Isle of Skye. The decision to lift the building off the ground on short concrete columns ensured that its footprint was minimal, releasing the designers from convention and allowing the house to relate to the wider context – the views to the north and the sun from the south. The form of the house was deliberately narrowed to the north, reducing its surface area, concentrating the view and leaning into the weather, while the cellular support spaces are clustered to the south. The lighthouse in the distance acts as a beacon to draw the focus of the house.

The entrance bridge lifts the visitor off the landscape and immediately upon entering one is drawn towards the fully glazed north elevation. Each of the windows on the other elevations has a particular role: the large high windows draw light into the two-storey volume while the smaller lower windows provide glimpses from the public side of the building and frame views to the west.

1   The house has spectacular views over the Isle of Skye

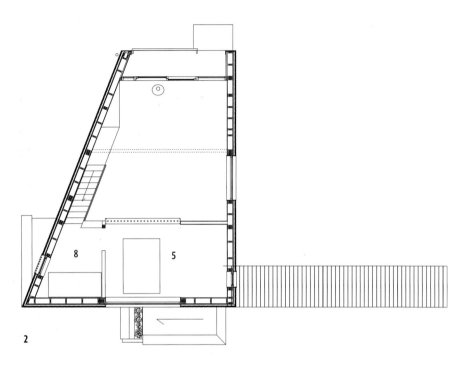

2

1 Entrance ramp
2 Deck
3 Living/dining
4 Kitchen
5 Bedroom
6 Bathroom
7 Composting toilet
8 Studio space

3

The structure of the house is deliberately on display – a flying central beam stiffens the construction and provides scale to the large volume. The interior is clad primarily in oriented strand board (OSB), used to provide racking strength to the timber frame and retained as the finished surface. At less than 70 square metres (750 square feet), space is at a premium, so built-in plywood furniture was designed to incorporate storage and the stairs that lead to the upper level. The house was stick-built on site by local tradespeople, avoiding the need to import any materials. Little heating is required due to the high levels of insulation and the house has a minimal impact in the wider environment.

External detail was consciously avoided, not in the sense of minimalism but for a contemporary rustic simplicity. The roof is clad in corrugated agricultural sheeting with a tight verge detail to emphasise the simple form of the house. The texture and the rhythm of the Scottish larch boards provide a rigour to the exterior; the finish has now weathered to a silvery grey and folds of colour announce the entrance and frame the view.

8   Kitchen

9   The house is heated by a wood-burning oven

10   Plywood stair

11   Sleeping loft

PHOTOGRAPHY: ANDREW LEE PHOTOGRAPHER

1

HILL House

Nova Scotia, Canada

MACKAY-LYONS SWEETAPPLE ARCHITECTS

At first glance the Hill House appears to be audaciously sited atop a glacial hill, or drumlin, along Nova Scotia's southern shore. However, its hilltop courtyard responds to the traditional pattern of hilltop farms found throughout Lunenburg County, where a microclimate is formed by the simple pinwheeling siting of house and barn. As a result the house 'cultivates' rather than consumes the landscape. It merges with the hill with respectful confidence. The siting integrates both natural and cultural landscape geometries.

The house is aligned on the north–south axis of the 250-year-old agrarian pattern, while the diagonal path through the courtyard follows the long northwest axis of the drumlin left by the glacier 15,000 years ago. While the house acts as a 360-degree panopticon, its courtyard and battered 'haunches' offer protection in a harsh climate.

1   Pavilions frame the microclimate

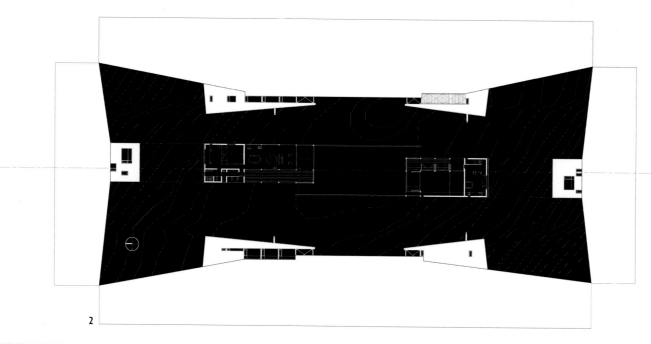

2 Plan and elevations

3 House as camera for a landscape photographer

4 Hilltop courtyard house offers both prospect and refuge

5 Guest house

6 Great room

PHOTOGRAPHY: STEVE EVANS (1, 3–6); MACKAY-LYONS SWEETAPPLE ARCHITECTS (2)

The program for this 280-square-metre (3000-square-foot) three-bedroom house consists of the main house with studio, a barn with guest quarters, and a courtyard garden between. Two low millwork and concrete walls uncoil from the two structures to embrace the courtyard. Together, the house and barn pinwheel around a central courtyard axis. The social space and barn face inwards to the courtyard through covered porches, while private spaces are stacked at the outer edges of the project. 'Served' and 'servant' functions are clearly articulated. This is a project that aspires to absolute conceptual clarity within minimum means.

The Hill House expresses the material culture traditions of the Maritimes. It embraces a long tradition of light timber framing and taut-skinned building envelopes, resulting in an architecture that is, paradoxically, both massive and delicate. This cultural sustainability is reinforced by hydronic in-floor heating and the use of local renewable materials and craftsmanship, resulting in an accessible and affordable architecture.

1

HONG KONG Villa

Hong Kong, China | **OLSON KUNDIG ARCHITECTS**

Set on a rocky hillside overlooking the South China Sea, this house is designed to respond to the elements and provide views of the stunning coastal scenery. The design was inspired by traditional Chinese architecture and furniture.

Lead architect Jim Olson's design includes large expanses of glass revealing dramatic views in every direction. Seamless transitions from inside to outside merge the house with its landscape, while broad overhangs provide protection from the tropical sun and driving rains.

On the uphill side of the house, the formal entry is accessed via a large central courtyard that incorporates a reflecting pool. Flanking this dramatic central entry space are the more intimate portions of the house, the living and dining areas, with private quarters book-ending the single-level plan. A second pool runs along the ocean side of the house, visually merging with the water and the island-studded coastline in the distance.

1   **Deep overhangs, inspired by traditional Chinese architecture, protect the interior spaces from the harsh climate**

Interior finishes are concrete, Chinese limestone (sourced locally for the project), glass, wood and bronze. The use of similar colours in the interior and on the exterior allow the house to respond to the landscape. The dramatic central space with 7.5-metre (25-foot) ceilings is flanked by more intimate seating and dining areas. The custom furnishings in this grand space were designed to be masculine and substantial; in private areas, they are softer.

In a region focused mainly on efficient commercial buildings, the construction of a high-end residential home posed unique challenges for the contractors. The owner elected to have almost all the building materials and custom furniture shipped from Seattle to Hong Kong. Highly skilled craftspeople from the Pacific Northwest fabricated furnishings and finishes – filling over eight shipping containers – including custom-fabricated bronze architectural elements and a commissioned Deborah Butterfield horse. Artist Mary Ann Peters travelled to the site and painted a full-length wall mural in the gallery that crosses the central axis.

2   The house seen from the driveway approach
3   A reflecting pool helps to merge the house into the landscape
4   View across entry reflecting pool through living room to South China Sea beyond

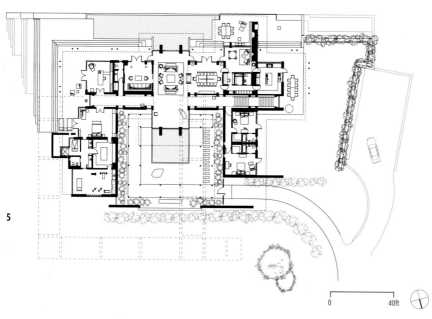

5

6

7

8

0   40ft

PHOTOGRAPHY: BENJAMIN BENSCHNEIDER

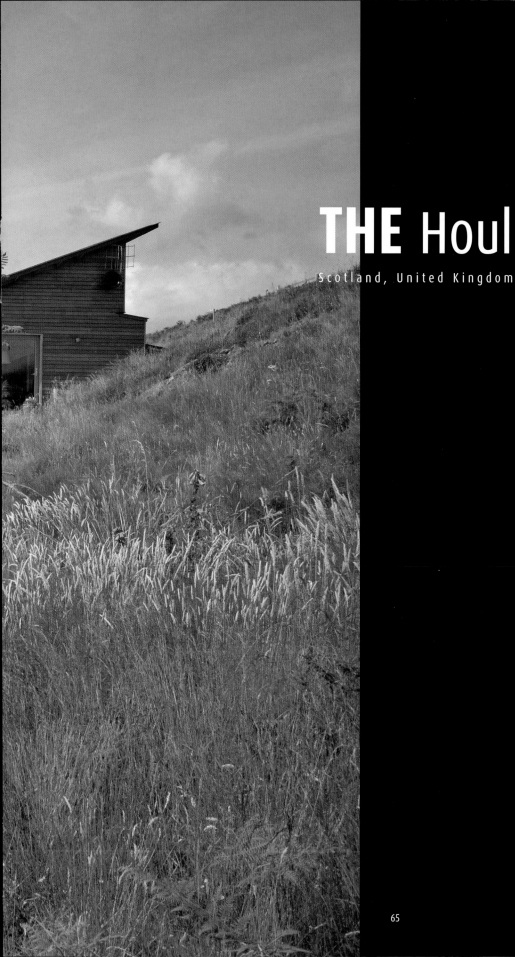

THE Houl

Scotland, United Kingdom

SIMON WINSTANLEY ARCHITECTS

The house is sited on a naturally concave hillside facing west to enjoy the spectacular view of the River Ken valley and the Rhinns of Kells hills beyond. It embodies current thinking about contemporary house design, including very low energy consumption (net zero carbon in this case) with very high levels of insulation, minimising air infiltration, heating by air-source heat pump, whole-house heat recovery ventilation and on-site generation of electricity by wind turbine.

The Houl is a single-storey long house with all principal rooms addressing the view and the ancillary service spaces to the rear. The slope of the roof of the main living accommodation follows the slope of the hillside. The roof of the ancillary areas meets the main roof at a shallower angle, allowing morning sunlight to penetrate the house through clerestory windows. The entrance is sited on the northeast side of the house under the cover of the roof to provide shelter from the prevailing winds.

1   **House in the landscape**

The construction has a galvanised steel and timber frame with walls clad in naturally weathered silver-grey cedar, triple-glazed windows and a roof finished with pre-weathered standing-seam zinc.

The galvanised steel frame is exposed externally on the main (west) elevation, with under-building walls set back to make the house appear to sit lightly on the ground. Galvanised steel was chosen for its aesthetic appearance combined with the cedar cladding, and for its long-term weather protection without the need for expensive paint covering.

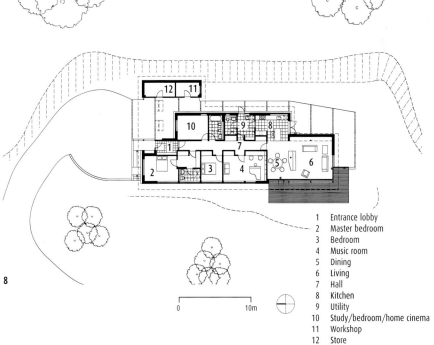
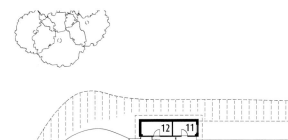

2   View to southwest over Ken valley

3   Dusk

4   Rear of house with clerestory windows

5   South gable showing slope of roof matching slope of hill

6   Front view of house and deck

7   House entrance

8   Floor plan

1   Entrance lobby
2   Master bedroom
3   Bedroom
4   Music room
5   Dining
6   Living
7   Hall
8   Kitchen
9   Utility
10   Study/bedroom/home cinema
11   Workshop
12   Store

0   10m

9   Dining / living space

10 Long gallery

11 Main living space

12 Kitchen

PHOTOGRAPHY: ANDREW LEE PHOTOGRAPHER (2–7, 9–12); SIMON WINSTANLEY (1)

HOUSE OF Passages

Central Jackson, Mississippi, United States

KEN TATE ARCHITECT

Offering a gentle journey from the street to the expansive views hidden behind its façade, this house poised on a lake in Mississippi provides release from the confines of daily life brought about by an unexpected encounter with nature's boundless beauty.

The first passage of this house – from the street into the private embrace of the courtyards – is marked by a wrought-iron gate illuminated by a glowing lantern. The gate opens into a courtyard where honey-coloured pavers surround an ancient fountain from France. Beyond, a fanciful façade combines iconic French provincial forms – a turret topped with a conical roof, sloping hip roofs, dormers with slate-covered caps – that seem to dance, projecting and receding to define irregularly shaped courtyards. Walking around the fountain, one is tempted to step through a wooden gate into a more intimate garden or through an iron one into the kitchen's herb garden, but the antique oak front doors, glazed with wavery glass, offer an irresistible invitation.

1   The house's shimmering reflection shows its intimate relationship with the lake

Within is a place of timelessness, where changes in material and style induce small shifts in mood from room to room. Paved with antique stone and topped with a barrel-vaulted ceiling, the entrance hall is a ceremonial space. In the dining room, lime-coated panelling of robust knotty pine detailed with stately mouldings is both rustic and refined. While the dining room's walls are wooden and its coved ceiling is plaster, this order is inverted in the living room, where massive oak ceiling beams crown plaster walls. Here, contemporary furniture with silvery upholstery shimmers in the light that flows through soaring arched French doors.

In a house full of passages, these doors mark the most dramatic one – a crossing from the house's shelter towards the lake's shining expanse. A classical loggia with a coffered ceiling and limestone columns celebrates the moment. Beyond, a stone terrace stretches towards the lake, ending with a thin reflecting pool that blurs the boundary between land and lake. At the pool's far edge, a fountain shoots jets of water that form a shimmering balustrade. The house's ultimate transition, this unexpected moment of whimsy invites surrender to the moment and the beauty of nature.

2   The round stair turret invites guests into the entrance courtyard

3   The loggia opens onto a terrace and fountain at the lake's edge

4   An antique fountain celebrates the entrance courtyard

5   An enfilade visually connects the kitchen, dining and living room

6   Limed beams and stone mantle highlight the tall living room

7   Antique, limed pine panelling creates a warm, inviting dining room

PHOTOGRAPHY: DAN BIBB (1, 2, 3, 5); TIMOTHY DUNFORD (4, 6, 7)

THE HOUSE of Planes /

1

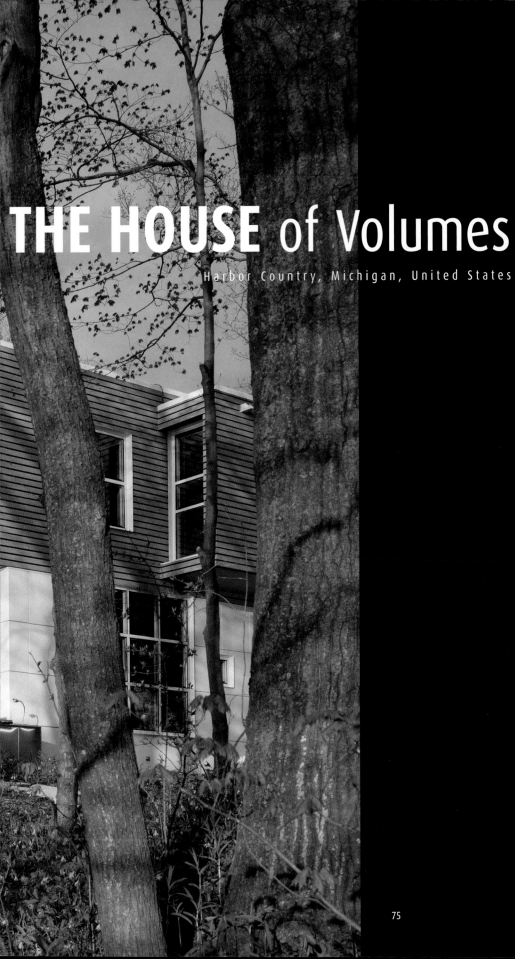

THE HOUSE of Volumes

Harbor Country, Michigan, United States

MARGARET McCURRY WITH STANLEY TIGERMAN

Design Team of the House of Volumes: Jeremy Hinton, Megan Musgrave
Design Team of the House of Planes: Jeremy Hinton, Rachel Oleinick
Interior Design of the House of Volumes: Margaret McCurry, Megan Musgrave
Interior Design of the House of Planes: Mary Luby, Mary Luby Interior Design, Inc.

Located on a sandy bluff overlooking Lake Michigan's southeastern shore, these two 650-square-metre (7,000-square-foot) homes expand an existing historic family compound that dates to the early 20th century. The Chicago-based clients desired sophisticated yet sustainable designs that would incorporate the amenities associated with their urban lifestyles into these more relaxed country retreats.

The houses were sited such that each family would inhabit its own private space while the terraced land between the homes would offer a central gathering site for the extended family. Since the land slopes towards the bluff, the first floors of the houses are stepped incrementally to follow the contours. A fieldstone path axially bisects this terraced area and terminates in a council ring, or fire pit, reminiscent of a favourite feature employed by Jens Jensen, the original landscape architect for the property. The partners also worked with the Michigan Department of Environmental Quality to carefully locate the houses to prevent dune

1   House of Planes (far left) with House of Volumes (right):
    view looking northeast from the Lake Michigan bluff

erosion. The plans incorporate wood boardwalks to traverse critical dune areas so that these slopes are preserved.

The two houses are each designed with a two-storey central circulation 'spline' that is flanked by living spaces. While acting as a transparent reveal between the forms, the spline contains the stairway thereby interconnecting the levels and linking the ground floor to family rooms below ground. Entry for each home is centred on the glazed spline, which sets up axial views through the double-height spaces onto rear patios and the lake beyond while flooding the stairwells with natural light.

Although each house is clad in mimetic materials, a rain screen of Port Orford cedar and white composite aluminium panels, each is also uniquely different in its material expression. For the House of Planes, the exterior walls are articulated such that they rise above and beyond the main volume of the structure while the floor planes extend beyond the walls to create deep balconies and overhangs. The house also shifts materials at each end to emphasise the 'slipped' planes. Its counterpoint is the House of Volumes, which is just that, stacked cubistic forms that are differentiated materially between the first and second storeys.

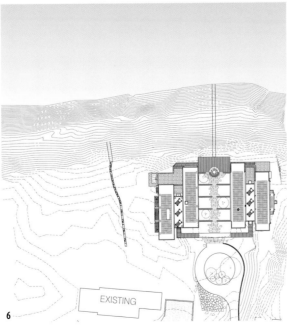

2&3 House of Volumes (left) and House of Planes (right): panoramic view looking west across Lake Michigan

4 House of Planes: north elevation

5&7 House of Planes (left) and House of Volumes (far right): rear view of terraces overlooking Lake Michigan

6 Site plan

EXISTING

0 80ft

House of Volumes

13

14

16

0   16ft

House of Planes

PHOTOGRAPHY: STEVE HALL © HEDRICH BLESSING PHOTOGRAPHERS

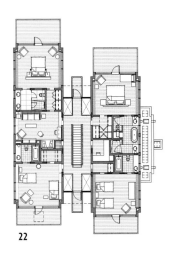

22

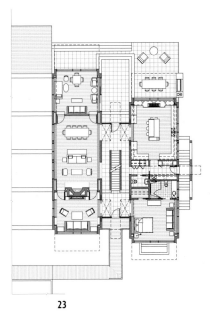

23

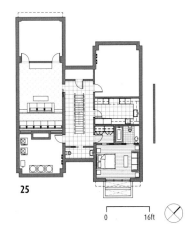

25

0   16ft

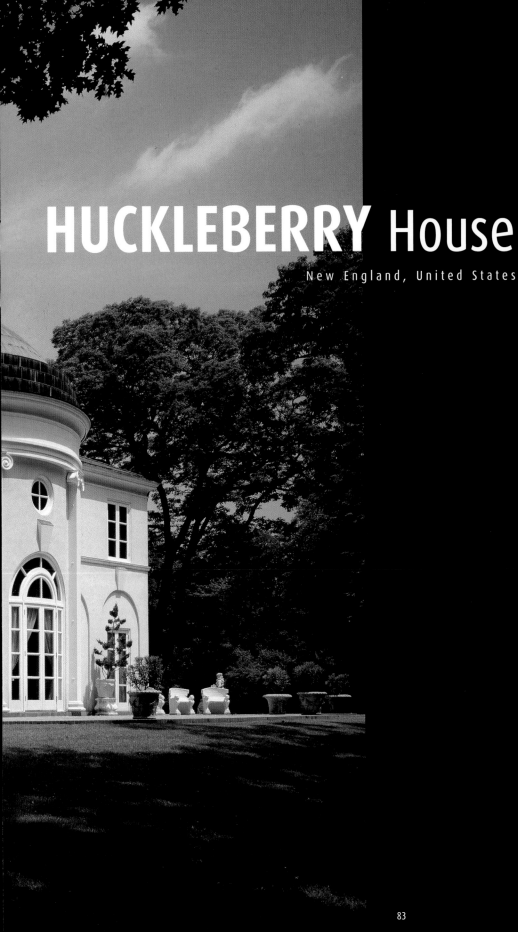

HUCKLEBERRY House

New England, United States

ALLAN GREENBERG ARCHITECT

This house was designed for a couple who love dancing and entertaining. The brief called for a two-storey domed ballroom and a plan that allowed for circulation through the first-floor rooms during parties.

The plan is arranged around two axes. The main axis bisects a sequence of symmetrical rooms: an enclosed entrance court, portico, vestibule, hall and ballroom. The cross-axis is arranged asymmetrically in a sequence of rooms that are themselves symmetrical. At opposite ends of the axis are a sunroom and a porch. The latter faces a swimming pool and a pavilion enclosed by evergreen hedges.

When the house was sold, the new owners asked Allan Greenberg to design an addition featuring a family room, additional bedrooms, and a study.

1   Garden elevation

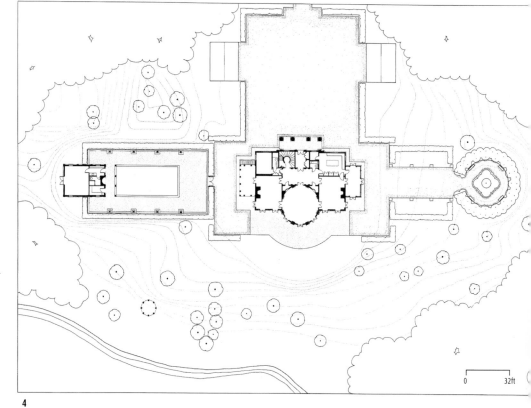

2   Front elevation with entrance court

3   Sunroom, facing southeast

4   Site plan

5   Interior, ballroom

6   Staircase

7   Detail of passageway

8   Passageway from original construction to addition

0   32ft

9   Pool elevation, northwest

10   Porch

11   View from porch towards pool and pavilion

12   Pavilion

PHOTOGRAPHY: TIM BUCHMAN (1–5, 9–12); JONATHAN WALLEN 6–8)

JASPERS' Loft

Brussels, Belgium | **MICHEL JASPERS**

In the old part of Brussels, in the lively heart of the city, this magnificent 680-square-metre (7300-square-foot) apartment is conceived as a loft with distinct living areas. Situated on the top storey of a historic building, it has a breathtaking view of the old streets and medieval roofs. A small stairway leads to a highly original covered roof-terrace providing a 360-degree bird's-eye view dominated by a stately, colossal courthouse that dates from the second half of the 19th century. A marble bust of King Leopold II emphasises the unmistakably Belgian milieu. The home also features a swimming pool, from which it is possible to enjoy the astonishing panorama even while swimming.

The home is part of a large-scale restoration project of the former Jacqmotte coffee-roasting factory, which had fallen into disuse since the 1970s. Converting the plant into a modern building – now housing several corporate headquarters, offices, conference centres, a restaurant

1   **Glass cube providing a 360-degree view over the historic part of Brussels**

and private flats of various sizes – was a significant challenge. The complex, now known as L'Espace Jacqmotte, is located in the Rue Haute in the legendary Les Marolles district, where the Flemish painter Pieter Brueghel the Elder lived in the 16th century.

2	The loft at the foot of the courthouse
3	Floor plan
4,5	Large windows provide a strong inside–outside experience

6   The entrance hall with statue of a lady welcomes visitors

7   Living and meeting area with a huge wall of colourful books

8   Kitchen

9   Looking in to the living area from the pool

10   Bathroom

11   Bedroom

PHOTOGRAPHY: TOM D'HAENENS AND THIERRY MALTHY

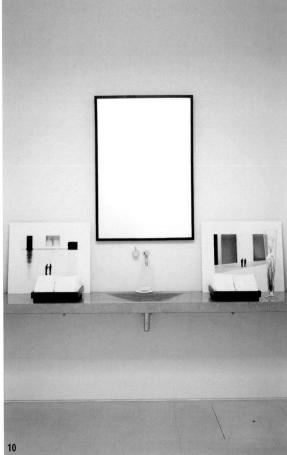

1

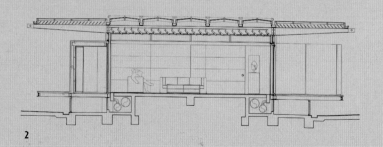

2

KAWANA House

Kawana, Japan | **FOSTER + PARTNERS**

The Kawana house, with its adjoining guesthouse, is one of several projects undertaken with the same client over a number of years. Early discussions focused on traditional Japanese architecture and were latterly distilled into a modern response. The result is a fusion of two traditions: the Japanese love of harmony and respect for nature and the Western refinement of a dematerialised architecture of steel and glass.

Sited on a dramatic stretch of volcanic coastline where long, inaccessible fingers of lava jut into Sagami Bay, the change in levels across the site and the views out to sea are central to the project's design. Set on a raised platform, the house is positioned so that the main living areas have uninterrupted views out to sea. Services and

1 The living space in the main house can be opened up to form a single volume, or subdivided by means of sliding screens
2 North–south section through main living space
3 North–south section through the guest house
4 North–south section through living and bedroom areas

storage areas are arranged around the perimeter, allowing the central accommodation to be configured as one continuous, open and flowing space. The framed structure creates seven rectangular bays defining the main spaces. These top-lit spaces can be subdivided by means of sliding screens, while adjustable louvres control the quality of natural light through the glazed roof. Full-height glazed sliding doors line the perimeter, allowing the living spaces to open out to adjoining terraces, thus eroding divisions between inside and out.

The surrounding landscape combines new elements with existing features. Mature trees line the cliff top, while newly planted camphor trees provide privacy from the road. Stone lanterns, some dating from the 8th century, are positioned around the house. A small teahouse of the late Edo period, brought from Shimane prefecture, completes the overall composition.

As a precursor to several future projects for the same client, the Kawana house laid the foundations for an enduring relationship that has enabled a profound exploration of traditional Japanese architecture in a modern context.

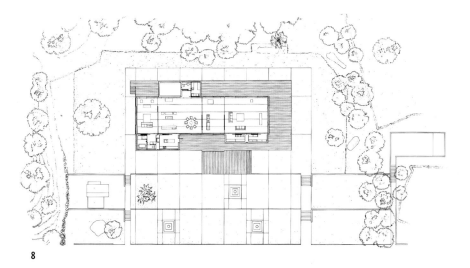

5 View of the south-facing terrace and pool of the guesthouse, built around a mature cherry tree

6 The master bedroom in the main house

7 The vista from the master bedroom along the length of the living space

8 Site plan

PHOTOGRAPHY: IAN LAMBOT

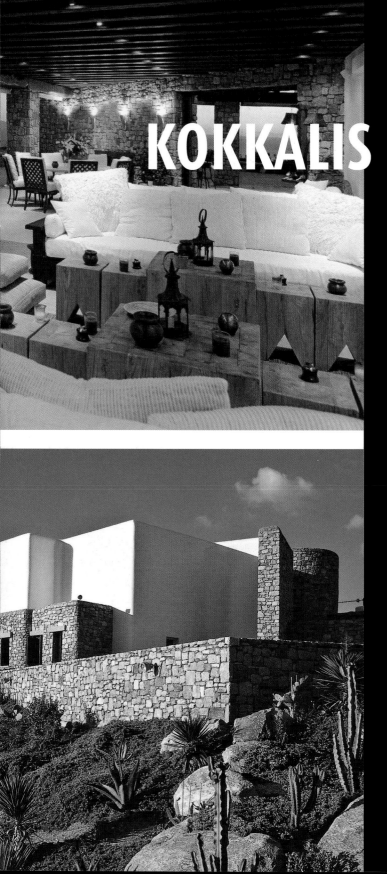

KOKKALIS House

Mykonos, Greece | **BC ESTUDIO**

From the outset, the forces of the various natural elements that converge in this enclave determined the design of the project. The unique geography, earthy colours, rocks, deep blue sea and bright white local architecture helped the architect uphold his basic architectural principles: respect for the environment and the integration of architecture into the landscape.

The summer residence consists of two buildings located on a rocky promontory overlooking the town of Mykonos and its port, from where it is possible to view the outline of several other Aegean islands. The two units were designed around a tower that is similar to an ancient fortress and are connected by stone walls. These walls organise the

1   Northwest façade
2   Main shade area
3   Infinity pool and bay view
4   West façade

outdoor spaces and create shaded areas, cliff-edge walks and an entrance along the pathway. The two houses face the sun and the views while remaining protected from northerly winds.

In order to improve integration and privacy, the rock found on the site was cut to adapt to the foundations of the house. From the entrance road the volume appears to have one level, but from the sea you can appreciate the different levels forming terraces. Common areas and the main suite are on the upper level, the guest rooms overlooking the pool and the bay of Mykonos are on the lower level. The interior design was carried out together with the owner, who opted for a mixture of antique and contemporary pieces. The courtyards feature Ancient Greek pots and enormous old oak-and-iron portals from the Xian dynasty.

5   Main entrance with view through to patio
6   Living space
7   Entrance lobby
8   Patio entrance
9   Site plan

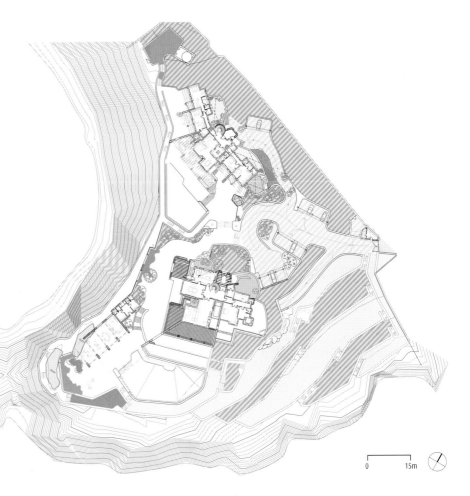

PHOTOGRAPHY: JULIA KILIMI (3, 4, 6–8, 10–15); PANAGIOTIS FOTIADIS (1, 2, 5)

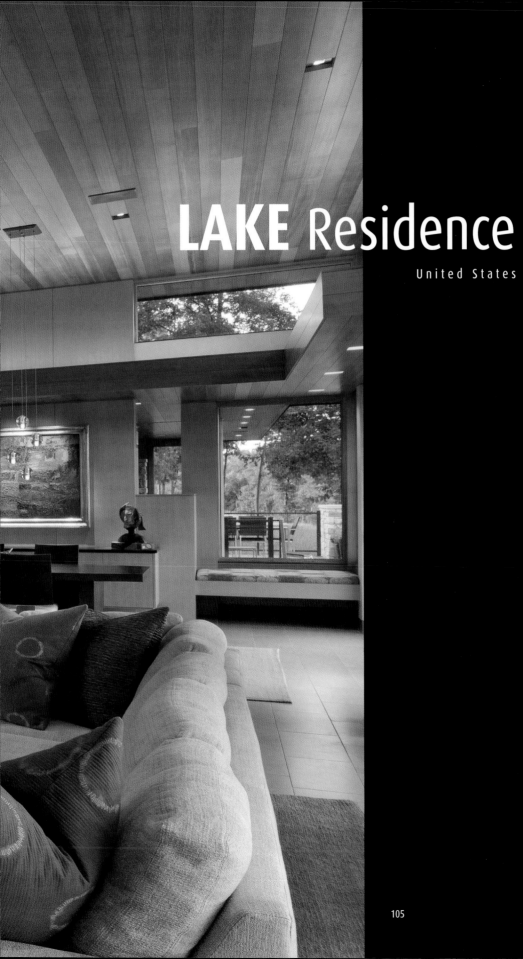

LAKE Residence

United States | **CHARLES R. STINSON ARCHITECTS**

Warm, yet elegant and modern, was the client's brief for this family home overlooking a serene lake. In response, the design team created a composition of wood and copper horizontal planes balanced by strong vertical forms of local limestone. A nuanced understanding of human scale – how the proportions of a space contribute to a feeling of comfort – along with CRS Interiors' organic material palette for the inside of the home, helped to fulfil the owner's desire for a feeling of warmth.

The extensive use of high-performance windows optimises views of the lake and ensures that sunlight reaches every room throughout the seasons. This design feature has the additional benefit of providing the occupants with the sensation of floating on the lake, almost as though they are living on a beautiful yacht.

1   The open floor plan is synonymous with the owners' lifestyle

This four-bedroom home is both a family retreat and sanctuary; a place for family members to reconnect with each other as well as the natural environment. Reflecting the characteristically positive nature of its designer, the house provides a harmonic balance between a sense of shelter and an openness that allows the spirit to soar.

2   The home nestles within the landscape

3   All windows are operable in the four-season porch

4   The interior designer, CRS Interiors, developed a warm interior material palette

5   Horizontal and vertical planes define the front entry

6   Wood ceilings and accent walls offer a feeling of warmth

7   Clerestory windows bring in light throughout the day

8   The interiors are designed to be in harmony with nature

9   The master bathroom is a tranquil retreat

10   The kitchen is a functional yet elegant centre to the home

PHOTOGRAPHY: PAUL CROSBY

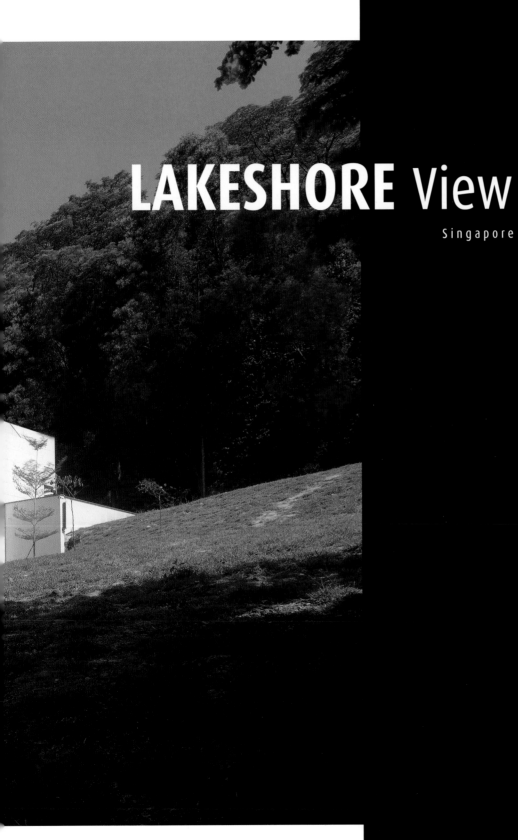

LAKESHORE View

Singapore | **SCDA ARCHITECTS**

Located on the highest hillside parcel overlooking the nearby golf course and port shoreline, Lakeshore View House addresses the potential of a sloping site using a composition of volumes. The design meets the client's brief while creating a flow of formal and informal interconnected spaces.

Fit to the contours of the site, the house is revealed slowly on arrival, creating a sense of expectation. A series of terraced water courts unifies the space within the building's central axis, flowing from a quiet reflective pond on the upper levels down through stepped landscaping, eventually reaching the poolside level where a panoramic viewing deck lines the length of a cantilevered, acrylic-edged swimming pool.

The two wings of the house reflect the need to delineate separate spaces for entertaining and more private living

1   The two main programs of the house – the entertainment area and the private living area – are expressed as two floating boxes; the pool cantilevers and is edged with 50-millimetre acrylic slabs

2 The volume of the house cantilevers over the rusticated black granite walls; the narrow zone on the left houses a straight flight staircase

3 The cantilever at the second level hovers above an acrylic-edged swimming pool

4 Pool and deck with panoramic view to the city

5 The rusticated dark-grey stone base presents a stark contrast to the light coloured cantilevered boxes

6 The private study looks into a water court with an external stair leading to the roof terrace

zones. The master wing, with a private study and master bedroom placed slightly off axis, cantilevers at the third storey over the pool and patio. It is connected to one end of the poolside patio via the double-volume private living space. The main living space is accessed from the patio and its upper foyer frames views of the surroundings by way of a system of 6.8-metre-tall (22-foot-tall), double-volume glazed panels. The base of the house contains additional living areas, a pantry and bedrooms that open to a deck with continuous seating and an adjoining lawn.

The house uses a contrast of white aluminium cladding panels to express the transparency and interconnectivity of the upper levels, while rough dark-grey granite forms the base foundation and footing of the house. The built massing is broken down by the interplay of shade louvres and trellises with thin aluminium extrusions articulating the façade openings. The central terraced water court entry unveils the relationship between the building and its site, with the journey ending upon arrival at the poolside patio, which frames and reflects panoramic views of the natural surroundings.

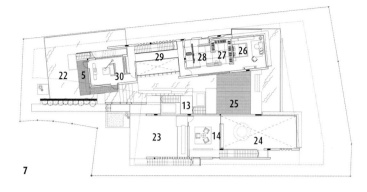

7

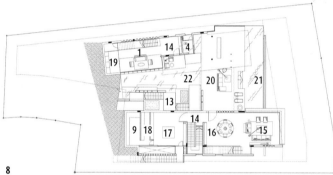

8

9

10

11

0　　　　　5m

1　Family
2　Bedroom
3　Gallery
4　Powder room
5　Patio/deck
6　Yard
7　Maid's room
8　Maid's bathroom
9　Storage
10　Utility
11　Household shelter
12　M&E room
13　Landing/planter
14　Foyer
15　Living
16　Dining
17　Kitchen
18　Pantry
19　Wine cellar
20　Pool deck
21　Swimming pool
22　Reflective pool
23　Car porch
24　Open to below
25　Timber clad roof
26　Master bedroom
27　Walk-in robe
28　Master bathroom
29　Glass bridge
30　Study

7   Second floor plan

8   First floor plan

9   Basement floor plan

10   View of the two-storey living space from the stairs

11   The internal elevation of the windows in the living room is lined and finished with vertical glass fins

12   The family room looks out to a water court and is located under the glass bridge

13   View of master bathroom

14   View of the glass bridge connecting the family and bedroom area

PHOTOGRAPHY: MR. AARON POCOCK

1

2

4

3

5

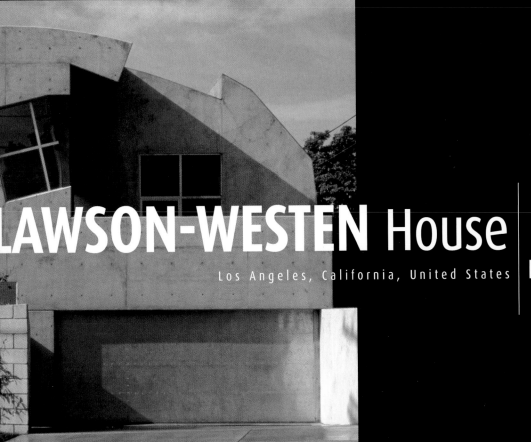

LAWSON-WESTEN House

Los Angeles, California, United States | **ERIC OWEN MOSS ARCHITECTS**

The house is positioned on the north side of a 25- by 55-metre (80- by 180-foot) suburban site, creating an L-shaped garden on the south side and west end. The clients' very particular building programme was a thoughtful reflection of how they live day to day, and how the housing of their substantial art collection should interrelate with the resolution of their practical concerns.

The kitchen, an entertainment and gathering space for family and friends, is the social centre of the home. Its three-level cylindrical volume – sometimes closed, sometimes open – contains the first-floor dining and cooking areas, with living spaces of various types attached to the open volume on the first, second and third floors.

1   West elevation and garden
2   Exterior detail of corner window
3   Physical model, west elevation
4   South elevation, entrance
5   Street view showing southernmost poured-in-place concrete wall

A second-floor walkway connects the adults' sleeping area – which is adjacent to the cylinder on the west – with the children's sleeping area at the east end of the house. The bridge passes above and through the triple-height living room, then proceeds through the second level of the cylinder to the adults' bedroom and bathroom. Within the cylinder, the bridge meets a stair that rises – following the profile of the cylinder wall and hanging out over the kitchen and living room areas – to a third-floor study at the top of the cylinder. Another stair, following the curve, leads up to a small outdoor deck.

The street-facing façade is poured-in-place concrete, while the remainder of the exterior building walls are smooth cement plaster. The building investigates window types, and represents those types as an assembly of windows – a single large window made of a number of pieces – on the south elevation next to the garden. This window represents, in the aggregate, all the window types that are found singly elsewhere on the exterior walls of the structure.

Geometrically, the centre of the cylinder's conical roof shape is not synonymous with the centre of the cylinder. This explains why the intersection between the cone roof and cylinder is a line that rises and falls, rather than the horizontal line that would separate the two if their centres were the same.

6   North elevation, backyard
7   Conical roof and intersecting cylinder shaft beyond
8   Spiral stairwell leading to outdoor deck
9   Triple-height living area, kitchen and dining beyond

10   Site plan, first and second floors

11   View from second-floor bridge; cone and cylinder intersect

12   View down to kitchen from top of cylinder

13   Master bedroom

14   Second-floor bridge connecting to stair that follows profile of
     cylinder wall

PHOTOGRAPHY: © ERIC OWEN MOSS (3, 10); © TOM BONNER (1, 2, 4–9, 11–14)

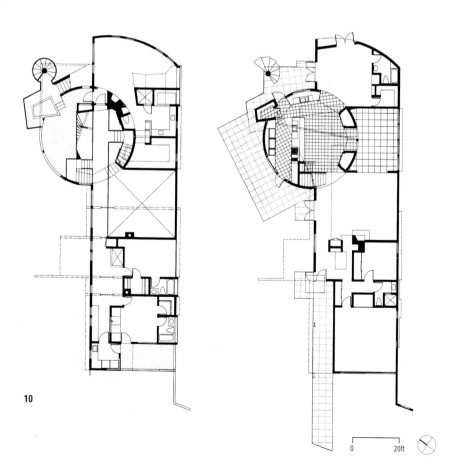

10

11

12

LINEAR House

Salt Spring Island, British Columbia, Canada | **PATKAU ARCHITECTS**

Located on a 6.5 hectare (16-acre) farm on Salt Spring Island, the site of this 340-square-metre (3700-square-foot) house is bisected from east to west by a long row of mature Douglas fir trees. The southern half of the property is an orchard containing a variety of fruit trees and the north half of the property is a hay field.

The house extends 85 metres (270 feet) in a straight line along the south side of the fir trees and is subdivided by a breezeway into a principal dwelling and guest quarters. The exterior is clad in charcoal-coloured fibre-cement panels, which render the house almost invisible when seen against the dark foliage of the firs.

Interiors are described by a luminous inner lining of translucent acrylic panels. More than forty skylights bring sunlight into the roof and wall assemblies during the day, causing the interior lining to glow softly; while at night,

1   **North-side kitchen opening with glazing retracted**

fluorescent lights mounted within the skylight openings turn the entire interior into an incandescent field. Areas within this surround are subdivided and defined by the insertion of reinforced concrete fireplace masses and wood cabinet-like service spaces. Retractable glazed doors allow the house to be transformed into an open-air pavilion in fair weather.

2   North side detail

3   West elevation

4   Breezeway looking north

5   Master bedroom with glazing retracted

6   Kitchen entrance

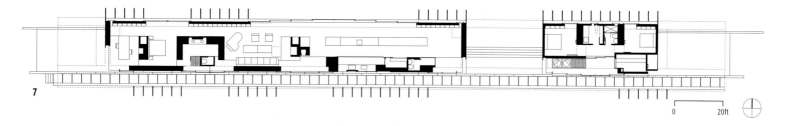

7

0   20ft

8

7   Floor plan

8   Kitchen with glazing retracted

9   Main fireplace

10   Master bathroom

11   Guest bedroom

PHOTOGRAPHY: JAMES DOW

LYLE House

Dalton, Georgia, United States | **WILLIAM T. BAKER**

One of the most extensive country estates in its region, the Lyle Estate is anchored by an English-style manor house. Situated on 80 hectares (200 acres), the house and its landscaped grounds are a perfect composition of what a great estate should be.

The setting for the main house, on a raised bluff with a western exposure to the horizon, is ideal. The driveway winds its way through the woods until it breaks out onto a large meadow. The drive follows the edge of the meadow until it curves and reveals a glimpse of the house in the distance. Thus, the estate reveals itself in stages, creating a progression of discovery.

The main house is constructed of Tennessee fieldstone, Indiana limestone and Vermont slate. The English-style manor house greets its guests with a rose-covered stone entryway that leads to the massive wood doors with their hand-forged iron strap hinges. The doors open to reveal

1   Aerial view

the dramatic surprise of a two-storey oval foyer with a curved stair leading the eye up to the panelled elliptical dome above. To the right is the home's living room with its antique Carrera marble mantle and the owner's collection of musical instruments. To the left of the foyer is a spectacular dining room with a hand-painted custom wall covering that was imported from China. The highly detailed cornice complements the elegant furnishings, china and crystal. The long gallery hall across the back of the home leads to a two-storey panelled library at one end and a kitchen and family area at the other. A private garden is located just through the tall stone mulled window. In the centre of this garden, an armillary sphere keeps track of time.

5 Second floor plan

6 First floor plan

7 Gallery hall

8 Main living room with collection of musical instruments

9 Kitchen and family area

10 Lounge

11 Trellised walkway through to fountain

PHOTOGRAPHY: JEAN CARNET (1); JAMES LOCKHART (2–4, 7–11)

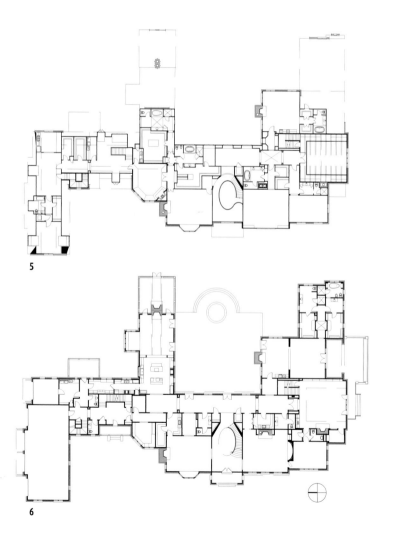

5

6

7

8

MASSACHUSETTS House

| **CBT ARCHITECTS**

The owners of this residence wished to create a second home in the mountains of western Massachusetts where they could vacation with their two grown children. The rural environment and the use of the house as a vacation 'cottage' suggested employing simple geometric profiles for its expression. The form and arrangement of spaces within the home take advantage of sunlight and views of the surrounding Berkshires and achieve a logical circulation flow with an appropriate separation of public and private spaces.

1   The house is securely rooted in the sloping mountainside – its shape and fenestration responding to and expressing the distinctive nature of the space within

2   View from the east looking out over the valley

3   View from the south entrance side: the tower provides panoramic views of the countryside

4   The entrance provides a protective transition from the natural environment to the more formal spaces within

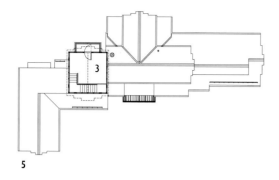

5

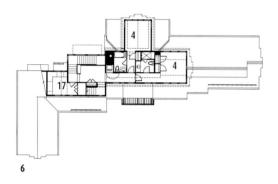

6

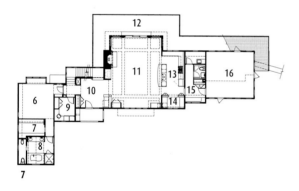

7

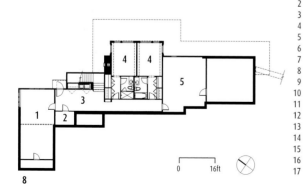

8

1 Game room
2 Wine cellar
3 Sitting area
4 Bedroom
5 Storage
6 Master bedroom
7 Closet
8 Master bathroom
9 Laundry
10 Foyer
11 Great room
12 Deck
13 Kitchen
14 Pantry
15 Mudroom
16 Screen porch
17 Study

0   16ft

The house is sided in red cedar shingles arranged with two wide bands alternating with a narrow one, creating a broader overall shingle pattern in scale with the size of the house. The sloping roof, typical for climatic conditions in the northeast, significantly impacts the sculptural form of the house. The stepped roof forms help mitigate the overall size of the house by articulating smaller-scaled pieces. Simultaneously, the roof shape helps reinforce the clarity of the floor plan by expressing the volume and organisation of interior spaces and, through the manipulation of eave height and overhang, conveys a pleasing form and a sense of protective shelter.

The tower, rising vertically from the centre of the house, acts as a marker identifying the location of the main entrance. A private, quiet room for the owners is set high above the ground at the top of the tower to take maximum advantage of the panoramic views. The tower also helps ventilate the home, cooling the house in the summer by

5   Fourth floor plan

6   Third floor plan

7   Second floor plan

8   First floor plan

9   The screen porch, with its roof monitor, captures the southern light and opens onto a grass terrace with shading trees

10 The living area, with its indigenous stone fireplace and beamed ceiling opens onto a cantilevered deck with vistas to the surrounding countryside

11 The living area with its corner windows providing a panoramic view of the valley below

venting warmer air out and allowing cooler air to be drawn in below. A screened porch and terrace are positioned on the right side of the home to take advantage of the southern orientation and to connect to the activities of the kitchen. A deck leads from the living area to the terrace.

12 The screened porch from within: glass panels replace screens to provide extended use in cooler weather and protection during snowy winter months

13 Although open to the activities taking place within the living area the kitchen is treated as a distinct space, an alcove adjacent to the living area

14 Large glass areas designed for the southern side of the house capture the changing sunlight and provide views up the mountainside

15 The master bedroom with a window seat and views out over the valley

PHOTOGRAPHY: RICHARD MANDELKORN

15

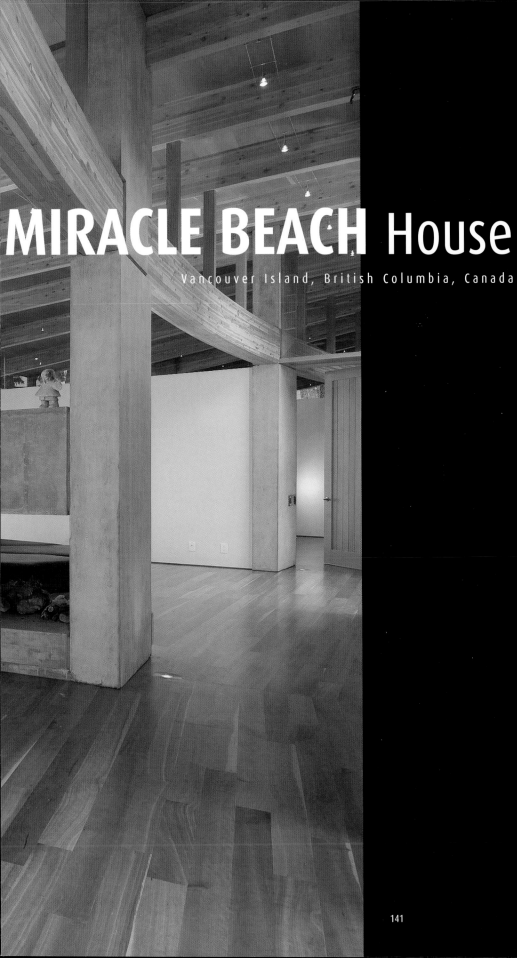

MIRACLE BEACH House

Vancouver Island, British Columbia, Canada

HELLIWELL + SMITH • BLUE SKY ARCHITECTURE INC.

Planned as a sweeping crescent-shaped structure open to spectacular ocean and mountain vistas, this 425-square-metre (4600-square-foot) house with a 53-square-metre (570-square-foot) studio was built as a gathering place for an extended family living in England and Canada, on a 3-hectare (7-acre) oceanfront site on the eastern shore of Vancouver Island. The convex northern side of the house looks over a pebble beach across Georgia Strait to the Coastal Mountains. The concave southern side forms a protected garden courtyard that embraces the sun.

Inside, sculptural timber roofs float above walls of glass and cedar. Fir beams curve through the spaces, highlighting a circulation gallery and invoking a sense of curiosity as to what lies beyond. These beams support a series of undulating rafters that define and form sensual, sculptural spaces. Curving beams tie into vertical concrete fins that

1   Dining room

provide a sense of gravity and tectonic syntax. All sheer forces are resolved into these cast-concrete monoliths, exposed on the interior and clad in large bluestone slabs on the exterior.

The interior is sparsely detailed with simple wall planes, hardwood floors, architectural concrete and bluestone details. A transparent link with folding glass walls creates the illusion of two homes, one for four teenage boys and one for their parents. A series of 1.5-metre by 2.75-metre (5-foot by 9-foot) pivot doors open towards the shoreline. The plan arcs continue outside as a formalised and unifying landscape element between the buildings, gardens, forest and sea.

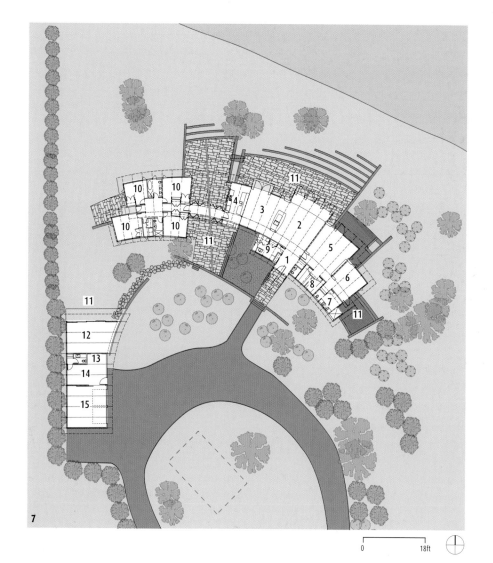

1	Entrance
2	Living room
3	Dining room
4	Kitchen
5	Main bedroom
6	Gym
7	Ensuite
8	Office
9	Utility
10	Bedroom
11	Terrace
12	Studio
13	Mechanical
14	Storage
15	Garage

7	Site plan
8,9	Great room
10	Kitchen: great room
11	Master bathroom

PHOTOGRAPHY: GILLIAN PROCTOR PHOTOGRAPHER (1, 8–11) PETER POWLES
PHOTOGRAPHER (2–6)

1

MODERN Classical House

Hampshire, United Kingdom

ROBERT ADAM,
ADAM ARCHITECTURE

Situated on a 285-hectare (700-acre) working farm in Hampshire, this major new country house of over 1400 square metres (15,000 square feet) includes 10 bedrooms, a series of state rooms, a family wing, a farm office, garaging and staff accommodation.

The house is both a traditional classical composition and an innovative design for a modern home. The unique but scholarly interpretation of classical architecture is combined with a strict geometry to create a striking new house. Double-height classical columns frame large windows and fine stone carving highlights restrained stone façades. The composition is influenced by famous classical designers from the past, such as 'Greek' Thompson and Friedrich Schinkel, but is unmistakably contemporary.

The house is planned with the same rigour as the façades while reflecting the particular functional requirements of the family. The main entrance and major reception rooms

1   Entrance façade

147

PHOTOGRAPHY: JOHN CRITCHLEY

are all contained within the high cubic Bath stone building. The major rooms are set either side of a series of geometric top-lit spaces culminating in a dramatic domed circular cantilevered stair. The informal family accommodation is in a lower wing of buff brick arranged around a small courtyard, composed in the same manner as the main house but much simplified. Between the lower and higher wings, a linked square stone tower with a shallow copper dome houses the farm office. Beyond the family wing, a long garage and service building with staff accommodation above creates a private courtyard with the family wing and tower.

The new parkland is on a secluded farm in the Hampshire countryside. The house commands a fine prospect over unspoilt rolling countryside with the nearby village hidden in a valley below. The house can just be seen from distant views but is immediately and impressively visible on entry to the new park. The approach is carefully organised to provide an immediate impact, but the house is then revealed gradually as the tower and house provide various picturesque vistas until the full cubic stone-and-glass façade is revealed on the final approach.

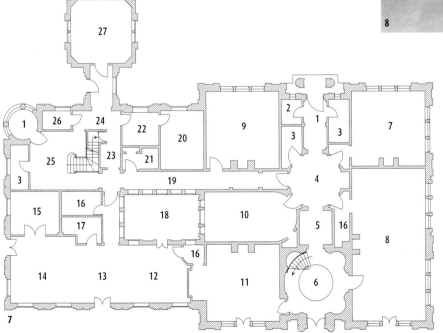

1	Vestibule	15	Nursery
2	Coats	16	Store
3	Cloakroom	17	Pantry
4	Octagonal hall	18	Courtyard
5	Inner hall	19	Corridor
6	Stair hall	20	Fishing/games room
7	Library	21	Lift
8	Drawing room	22	Utility room
9	Sitting room	23	Boot room
10	Billiard room	24	Office hall
11	Dining room	25	Hall
12	Kitchen	26	Bathroom
13	Breakfast	27	Office
14	Family room		

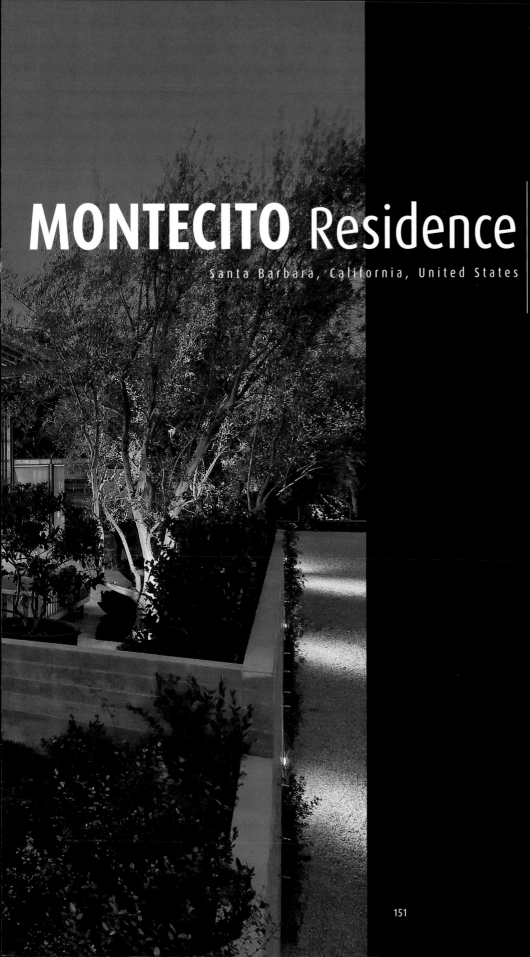

MONTECITO Residence

Santa Barbara, California, United States

BARTON MYERS ASSOCIATES

The Montecito Residence is situated in the secluded hills of Santa Barbara on half a hectare (1 acre) of environmentally sensitive habitat with dense vegetation and large boulders. The clients' ambition was to design a home with the clarity of an Asian space, the discipline of modernism and the visual warmth and textures of Mexico.

The home consists of a 280-square-metre (3000-square-foot) main residence, a 45-square-metre (500-square-foot) garage, a sun deck adjacent to a 15-metre (50-foot) pool and an existing guest house. The main residence is broken up into two wings: one includes the living and kitchen areas and the second includes the bedroom, bathrooms and library. The layout is influenced by the topography of the landscape, sited among protected oaks and large boulders. The buildings frame an intimate courtyard, allowing the rugged site to embrace the house, and maximise ocean vistas.

1   Pedestrian gate and staircase leading to the house

The residence is designed in the tradition of the architect's other steel houses with an exposed structural frame, overhead roll-up doors that integrate outdoor spaces, concrete floors, exposed decks and the addition of infill-insulated metal panels for the enclosure. The architect's ongoing residential explorations creatively envision a flexible prototype for mass-produced housing using steel construction and standardised off-the-shelf industrial components.

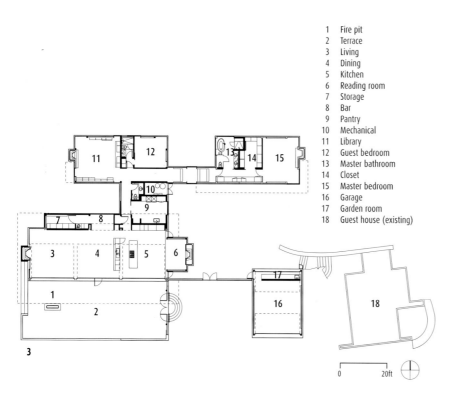

1   Fire pit
2   Terrace
3   Living
4   Dining
5   Kitchen
6   Reading room
7   Storage
8   Bar
9   Pantry
10   Mechanical
11   Library
12   Guest bedroom
13   Master bathroom
14   Closet
15   Master bedroom
16   Garage
17   Garden room
18   Guest house (existing)

0   20ft

2   Landscaped terraced gardens

3   Floor plan

4   View of the master bedroom corner

5   Mountain view from the dining room

PHOTOGRAPHY: CIRO COELHO

MORTLOCK LEE House

Girraween, Northern Territory, Australia | **TROPPO ARCHITECTS NT**

The Mortlock Lee House sits in a stringybark scrubland block sited around a large ironwood tree that provides a focus for the siting of the house.

Cruciform in plan, entering from the south, a lineal verandah extends into the bush as a platform to the north separating the main sleeping area from the house. The 72-square-metre (775-square-foot) house has a single roof pitching upwards to the south, which gives a light, airy internal volume. A generous lower awning to the north protects the walls from the sun.

The bathroom is placed at the entry to the house, allowing the visitor to slow down and refresh on arrival. The main bedroom has privacy from the house but is open to the bush. At the back of the living room and kitchen there is another sleeping area, which has been designed as one large space or two smaller spaces.

1   Large lineal verandah deck with bush views

2   Bush approach to large lineal verandah deck

3   Pool deck area

4   Pool deck edge detail

5   Inside–outside verandah living with minimal thresholds

The main structural frame is steel, galvanised for longevity and low maintenance. Australian hardwoods (some sourced locally) provide the substructure and flooring. A simple floor plan, section and structural system have allowed the house to be constructed by the clients as owner builders.

The protective 'hat' was designed to withstand torrential rains in the wet season and even cyclones, while also allowing cross ventilation in the heat. Designed to be tight, but just right, operable walls and window systems extend the experience of occupation, allowing indoor space to flow outdoors and vice versa – blurring the delineation of enclosure – the essence of Top End living.

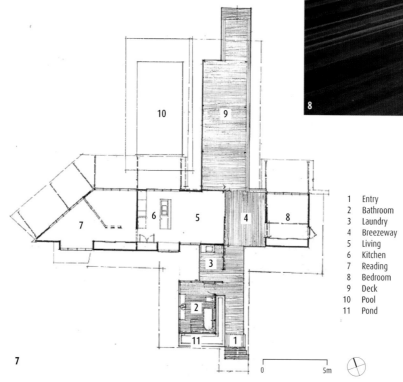

1	Entry
2	Bathroom
3	Laundry
4	Breezeway
5	Living
6	Kitchen
7	Reading
8	Bedroom
9	Deck
10	Pool
11	Pond

0   5m

6   Reading room

7   Floor plan

8   Living wing from breezeway

9   Shutter detail – high-level ventilation

10 Bathroom

PHOTOGRAPHY: PETER EVE, MONSOON STUDIO – PHOTOGRAPHY AND DESIGN

MOUNT DAVIS Villa

Hong Kong, China | **FARRELLS**

Located on the south side of Hong Kong Island overlooking the Lamma Channel, Mount Davis Villa is a home imbued with elegance, ingenuity and environmental sustainability. The villa is carefully placed within the site topography to maximise views and outdoor space while minimising road noise.

The narrow 600-square-metre (6400-square-feet) site is sandwiched between two busy roads and accessed via a steep driveway from the main road at the rear. The entry level has a single living area with a kitchen at its eastern end. Beyond that lie a partially covered lap pool and a games room, above which are the maid's quarters. The master bedroom, children's bedrooms and two bathrooms are on the second level. All the bedrooms have magnificent sea views and each room leads onto a terrace, created by 'cutting a slot' in the roof.

1   Solar panels power the air conditioning and 'slots' in the roof ensure each room has its own balcony

The villa is designed to utilise the latest environmental technologies. Air-conditioning for this 420-square-metre (4500-square-foot) house is powered by solar energy using an absorption-chiller system and is delivered through floor and ceiling vents. The system can be reversed to heat the house and swimming pools as necessary. There is also an integrated grey-water system, which collects, treats and purifies rainwater for lavatories and garden watering.

Inspired by a Malaysian long house, the building is arranged into two blocks contained under a single roof, a living area and a utility zone. The design is based upon three principal planes: the vertical stone wall, the horizontal timber deck and the inclined metal roof. These elements both control the composition and express a contemporary oriental design sense.

2　Challenging plot dimensions called for an under-house garage

3　The entrance wall features a stylish Heaven's Gate circular window

4　The villa's ingenious design combines luxury and eco-friendliness

5　Solar-powered reverse air conditioning heats the infinity lap pool, which overlooks the Lamma Channel

6　Living room and deck overlooking the Lamma shipping channel

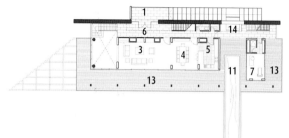

1	Entry stair
2	Family room
3	Living room
4	Dining room
5	Kitchen
6	Gallery
7	Gymnasium
8	Bedroom
9	Play room
10	Study
11	Swimming pool
12	Terrace
13	Deck
14	Spa/jacuzzi
15	Garage
16	Plant room

7	Third floor plan
8	Second floor plan
9	First floor plan
10	Basement plan
11	Master bedroom
12	Guest bathroom
13	Master bathroom
14	Floor-to-ceiling windows in the double-height family room flood the room with light and enhance the space

PHOTOGRAPHY: © CARSTEN SCHAEL

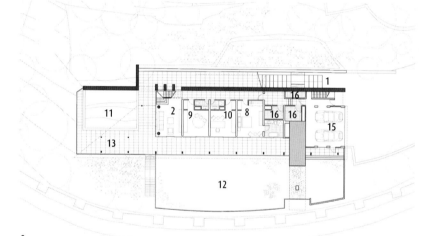

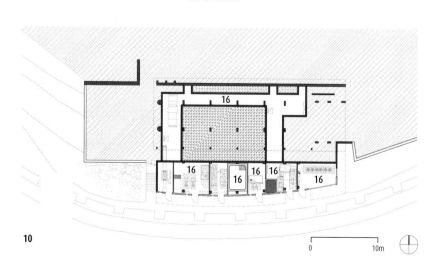

0   10m

1

OZ House

Silicon Valley, California, United States | **SWATT | MIERS ARCHITECTS**

The 850-square-metre (9,300-square-foot) OZ Residence in Silicon Valley captures the essence of casual California living with open planning, rich natural materials and a strong visual connection to beautiful gardens.

The owners, a couple with three young children, wanted their home to have a casual, barefoot feel – like a vacation destination. Their 1-hectare (2.8-acre) site, with gentle slopes to the south and mature landscaping on all sides, was the perfect setting to create a home that would engage fully with the beautiful landscape.

The design that evolved is based on a simple L-shaped plan with two wings. Connecting the two wings is a great room for living and dining, fully glazed on the north and south sides. The dramatic great room is a beautiful two-storey volume pierced by a skylight above that runs east–west and features a floating glass bridge connecting the two wings at the upper level.

1   Indoor–outdoor connection at entry

2   Entry at dusk

3   Great room with sunken living room and dining beyond

4   View from pool of the two-storey great room and south terrace

Deep, cantilevered roof extensions, sheathed in mahogany
boards at the central space and white stucco at the wings,
reinforce the overall horizontal composition, visually
dissolving the boundary between inside and outside.

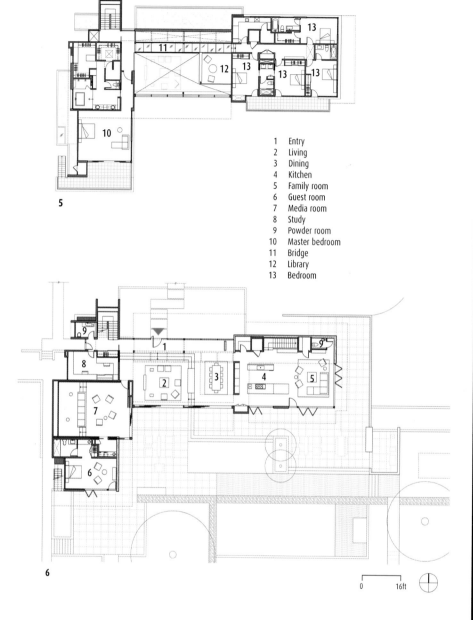

1	Entry
2	Living
3	Dining
4	Kitchen
5	Family room
6	Guest room
7	Media room
8	Study
9	Powder room
10	Master bedroom
11	Bridge
12	Library
13	Bedroom

0   16ft

5   Upper level floor plan

6   Lower level floor plan

7   Entry circulation with skylight and glass bridge above

8   Great room from below suspended library

9   Master bathroom

PHOTOGRAPHY: © TIM GRIFFITH

PADARO BEACH House

Carpinteria, California, United States

B3 ARCHITECTS

The goal for this 720-square-metre (7,800-square-foot) residence was to create a sustainable and multi-generational structure, bringing family together in separate enclaves within the residence. One challenge presented during the design process was to buffer noise created by the nearby freeway and the railroad track adjacent to the main entry of the site. This led to the creation of an interior courtyard to serve as a modern retreat from wind and exterior sound. The courtyard, inspired by the early California haciendas, creates a private oasis screened from neighbours, trains and traffic, and forms the core of the dwelling.

The home is sited with southern exposure in order to take advantage of solar gain in a cool ocean environment. Operable north-facing glass is utilised to facilitate thermal siphoning, creating air movement while exhausting any undue heat sink within the structure. By utilising recycled

1   Infinity pool overlooking the ocean

surfaces and reclaimed materials, the structure becomes a responsible dwelling with an energy performance exceeding California Energy Codes by 50 percent.

Careful attention was paid to the development of personal enclaves for extended family and guests alike. Separate wings and stairways provide residents with the independence to come and go as they please, and enjoy a variety of activities without disturbing each other.

This structure incorporates large glazed panels, melding exterior ocean vistas with interior environments.

1 Garage
2 Laundry
3 Bathroom
4 Kitchen
5 Breakfast
6 Dining
7 Great room
8 Music room
9 Media
10 Guest room
11 Multi-generational living
12 Courtyard
13 Multi-generational bedroom
14 Master dressing room
15 Master bathroom
16 Master bedroom
17 Open to below

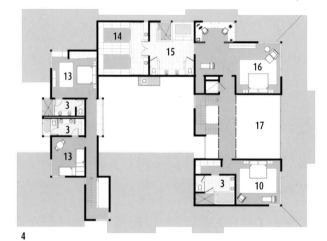

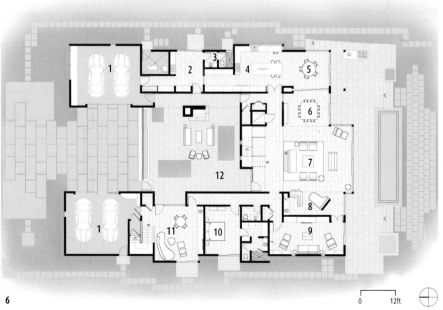

0   12ft

7   Enclosed interior courtyard sheltered from ocean breezes

8   A suspended interior bridge connects the master suite and guest suites, bisecting the living room

9   Mid-century furniture in the guest living area

10 The culinary centre of the house

PHOTOGRAPHY: CIRO COELHO PHOTOGRAPHY

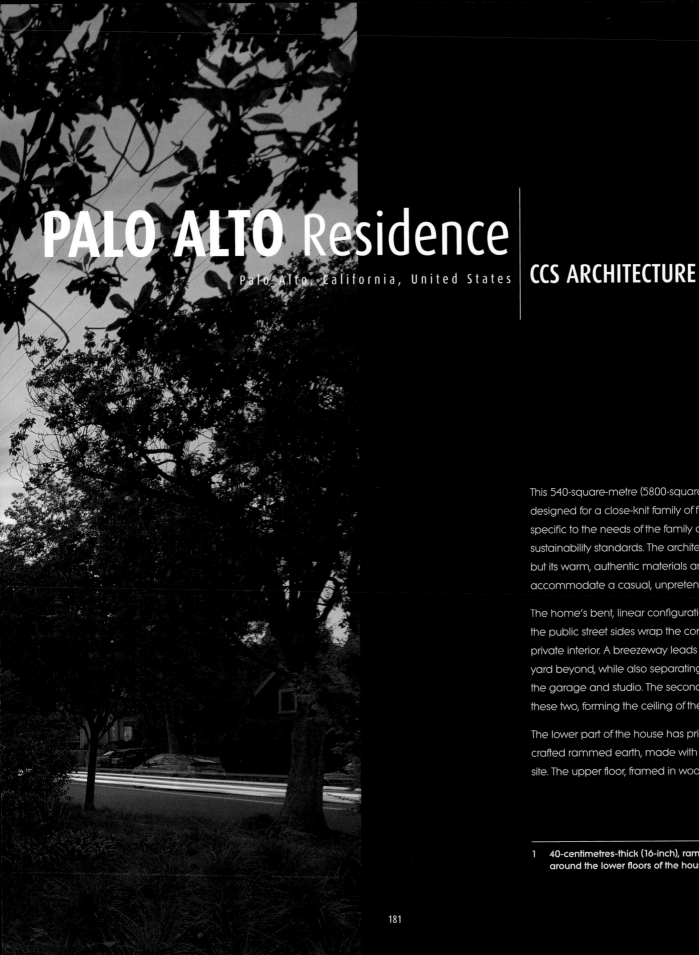

PALO ALTO Residence

Palo Alto, California, United States | **CCS ARCHITECTURE**

This 540-square-metre (5800-square-foot) home was designed for a close-knit family of five. The design is specific to the needs of the family as well as their rigorous sustainability standards. The architecture is contemporary, but its warm, authentic materials and refined details accommodate a casual, unpretentious lifestyle.

The home's bent, linear configuration divides the site; the public street sides wrap the corner, creating a more private interior. A breezeway leads to the entry and the yard beyond, while also separating the main house from the garage and studio. The second floor bridges over these two, forming the ceiling of the breezeway.

The lower part of the house has primary walls of highly crafted rammed earth, made with soil excavated from the site. The upper floor, framed in wood and steel, is clad in

1   40-centimetres-thick (16-inch), rammed-earth walls wrap around the lower floors of the house

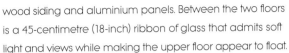

wood siding and aluminium panels. Between the two floors is a 45-centimetre (18-inch) ribbon of glass that admits soft light and views while making the upper floor appear to float.

The Genkan entry is a feature of many Japanese houses. Exterior stone paving extends into the entry, where shoes are removed, and the interior floor steps up 15 centimetres (6 inches). Living functions – including kitchen, dining, family room and office – inhabit the lower level, and all face a stone-paved courtyard with a Callery pear tree. The yard beyond is landscaped with a synthetic lawn and drought-tolerant meadow grasses. An L-shaped interior façade with 20 metres (65 feet) of wood-framed, sliding glass doors maximises the indoor–outdoor connection. Circulation is a continuous flow that emphasises the counterpoint between solid and open.

The second floor contains a library, three bedrooms and two bathrooms. A 25-metre-long (80-foot) 'gallery of light' connects the bedrooms and bathrooms; its skylights and windows are designed to animate the walls with geometric shapes derived from washes of light and shadow.

The stairway between floors is located where the house bends to form an angle. It leads up through an open space that connects the library above to the home office below, with natural light filtering in from the clerestory windows at the raised roof.

Across the breezeway is the garage/studio building. The studio is a general workspace, but it also has a full kitchen and bathroom for guests.

2   View of guest house, looking through breezeway towards street

3   Kitchen, dining, office and living spaces open completely to the interior courtyard

4   Landscaping comprises drought-tolerant plants and an artificial turf lawn

5   The previous home was carefully deconstructed to minimalise waste; about 50 percent of the material in the new rammed-earth walls is soil from the site

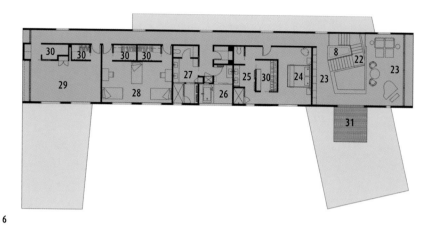

6

7

1	Entry	12	Garbage	23	Library
2	Shoe room	13	Laundry	24	Master bedroom
3	Bathroom	14	Dog wash	25	Master bathroom
4	Pantry	15	Breezeway	26	Spa
5	Kitchen	16	Garage	27	Kids bathroom
6	Dining	17	Guesthouse	28	Bedroom
7	Storage	18	Patio	29	Playroom/guestroom
8	Stair	19	Stone terrace	30	Closet
9	Office	20	Lawn	31	Deck
10	Living	21	Driveway		
11	Piano room	22	Planter		

6   Second floor plan

7   First floor plan

8   20 metres (65 feet) of wood-framed sliding glass doors maximise indoor/outdoor connections

9   The stairway leads up through an open space that connects the library above to the home office below

10 Home office; all wood is domestic hardwood

11 Dining space

12 Upstairs library and 25-metre (80-foot) 'gallery of light'

PHOTOGRAPHY: JOE FLETCHER, SAN FRANCISCO

POOL HOUSE Dubai

Dubai, United Arab Emirates | **CHAKIB RICHANI ARCHITECTS**

The villa is the main residence of a family with three young children in urban Dubai, close to the famous Burj Al Arab Hotel.

The programme includes an outdoor swimming pool, a large reception area and numerous indoor activities in addition to the private quarters and servants' facilities. The architects opted for an introverted scheme: the main spaces overlook the pool, which is landscaped as an oasis – a place of reclusion and serenity in the desert.

The main volume of the villa is a simple, plastered, rectangular prism connected to smaller volumes at each end by bridges. Rhythmical flying beams on the second floor connect the volumes visually and also flank the screen that separates the villa from the street. The flying entrance canopy, following the language of flying beams and bridges, is a striking feature in an otherwise discreet street elevation.

1   Flow of external space into patio and pool court

The pool elevation, on the other hand, is a plane of glazed openings connecting the interior and exterior. Sliding shutters of American red cedar protect the living spaces from the burning sun, casting ever-changing shadows.

The entrance lobby is a narrow, double-volume gallery with one blank wall washed with light from a skylight above. The strong perspective leads the eye to the corner window framing a small pebble garden with a long travertine bench – another quiet spot for relaxation. This gallery, which is overlooked by the corridor of the more private first floor, is the circulation spine opening onto the living and dining volumes.

The internal finishes are travertine and oak: neutral in colour, rich in texture. Many pieces of furniture and other accessories were chosen from the Chakib Richani Collection following the same design spirit.

2   Subdued street elevation, first skin layer, accentuated by the projecting canopy

3   Impressively high entrance door under floating canopy and flying beams

4   The 'Zen' pebble garden with long travertine bench

5   The swimming pool is the focus of the villa

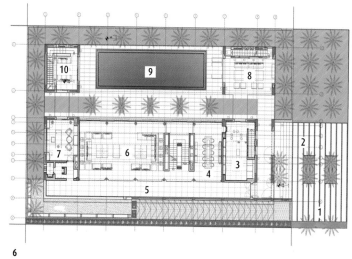

1 Car entrance
2 Entrance
3 Kitchen
4 Dining room
5 Gallery
6 Salon
7 Office
8 Patio
9 Swimming pool
10 Sitting room

6

7

6   Floor plan

7   Main living space: furniture designed by Chakib Richani Collection

8   Kitchen and family breakfast area

9   Games room with billiard table and bar area

10   Dining table, consoles and suspended lights designed by architects

PHOTOGRAPHY: CHAKIB RICHANI ARCHITECTS

RIVERBANK House

Melbourne, Victoria, Australia

JACKSON ARCHITECTURE
DARYL JACKSON

From its ideal situation on the banks of Melbourne's famous Yarra River, the Riverbank House enjoys stunning western views of the city's central business district. Upon entry, a sense of anticipation builds around what lies ahead.

The plan encourages the visitor to move through the various spaces sequentially. An indoor atrium garden awash with sunlight leads to a double-height living and dining space that overlooks a garden of existing mature trees. The trees provide a green screen for privacy as well as a foreground to the vistas of church spires, historic buildings, the botanical gardens and office towers beyond.

The bedrooms are accommodated on the level above, while a billiards room and recreation area are situated below the living spaces. A bridge spanning out towards the river, with a lap pool running below, links to an eyrie lookout, from which the verdant surroundings and stunning city views can best be appreciated.

1   White wall terraces cut into the hill, allowing the tennis court and orchard become outdoor rooms contiguous with the house

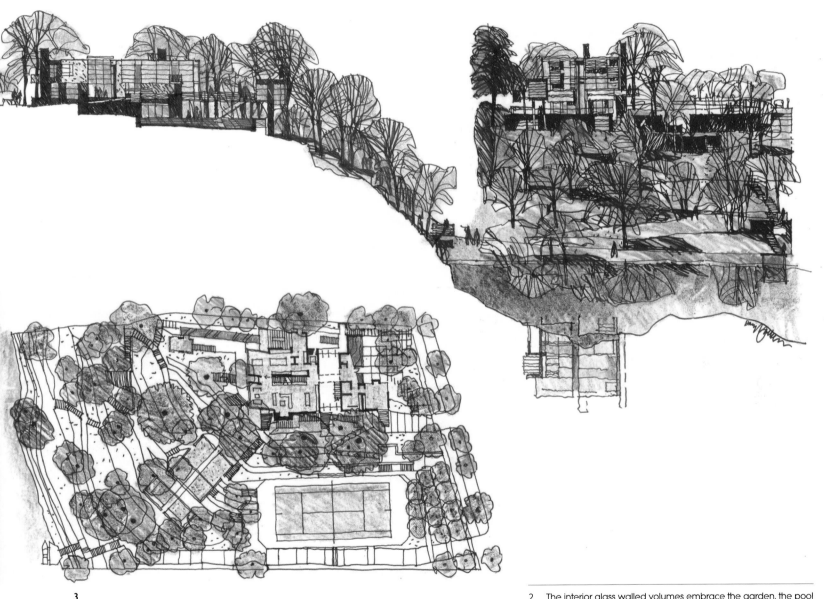

3

2   The interior glass walled volumes embrace the garden, the pool
    and the catwalk facing the city

3   A composite picture of the whole complex: house, garden and
    outdoor rooms, stepping down to the riverbank

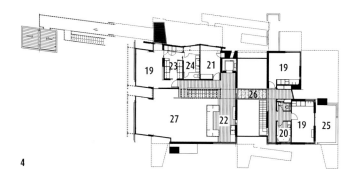

4

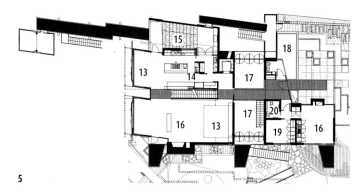

5

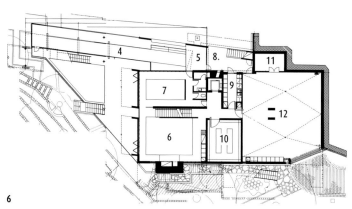

6

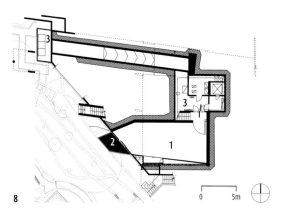

8

7

1	Gallery	15	Kitchen terrace
2	Balcony	16	Living
3	Plant room	17	Conservatory
4	Lap pool	18	Reflection pool
5	Pool house	19	Bedroom
6	Billiard room	20	Bathroom
7	Gym	21	Nursery
8	Laundry courtyard	22	Study
9	Laundry	23	Robe
10	Wine cellar	24	Ensuite
11	Wood room	25	Terrace
12	Garage	26	Bridge
13	Dining	27	Void
14	Kitchen		

0   5m

4   First floor plan

5   Ground floor plan

6   Basement one plan

7   Catwalk above pool, with eyrie above the garden beyond

8   Basement two plan

9   Street front and arrival via the terrace

PHOTOGRAPHY: GOLLINGS PHOTOGRAPHY

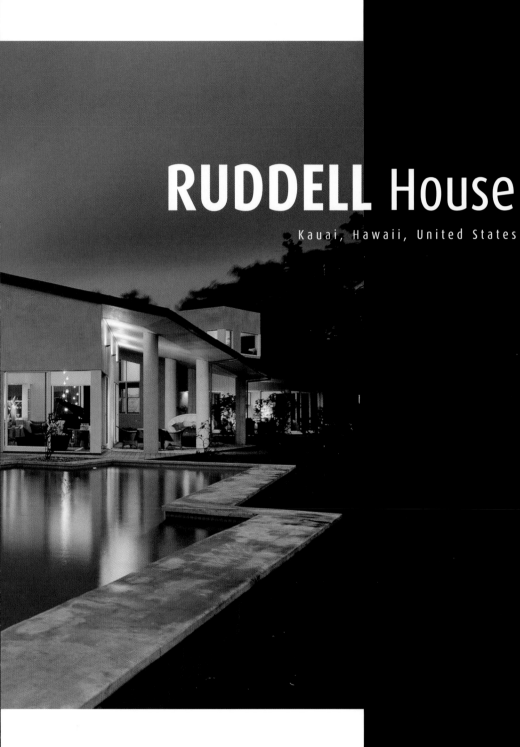

RUDDELL House

Kauai, Hawaii, United States

MOORE RUBLE YUDELL
ARCHITECTS AND PLANNERS

The Ruddell house is situated on the majestic north shore of Kauai and is shaped by the unique landscape characteristics of the island. The property is part of a working farm perched on the rim of a coastal valley, overlooking the dramatic coastline of the north shore.

Having recently moved from California, the clients longed to return to a place connected to the agrarian landscape. They imagined a home where they could live from their gardens and orchard, and host gatherings for artists, friends and relatives. In short, they wanted to live fully integrated with nature.

1   View looking east from the adjacent valley through Albizia tree forest
2   View looking west from adjacent terraced gardens
3   Passageway at the north wing leading to the pool terrace beyond; a second-level studio perches above the north master suite

Climate played a central role in the form and function of the house, situated on a southwest-facing bluff with valley and ocean views. The house is composed around the natural topography of the site and is organised as a series of pavilions, connected by loggia, courtyards and passageways.

The clients' desire for a union between inside and outside is realised in the way open spaces alternate with building masses along the circulation spine. Outside spaces vary in size, character and orientation. Thresholds between inside and outside are linked by patterns of movement and habitation.

The house functions to filter the trade winds, optimising natural ventilation and framing views. Deep overhangs provide shelter from the harsh tropical sunlight, while clerestory windows capture softer light.

The colour and material palettes reflect the dynamic colours of the sky and local flora, responding to the light and landscape to celebrate the cycles of nature. The building, landscape and inhabitants are woven into a dynamic yet harmonious composition.

4   Passageway at the north wing leading to the pool terrace beyond; a second-level studio perches above the north master suite

5   Western view at the main entryway

6   Southwest view from a secondary passageway looking towards the outside dining area

7   Second floor plan

8   First floor plan

1 Outdoor shower
2 Master sleeping bay
3 Closet
4 Master bathroom
5 Master bedroom
6 Outdoor dining
7 Storage
8 Outdoor kitchen
9 Garage
10 Outdoor deck
11 Dining
12 Living
13 Punea
14 Kitchen
15 Office
16 Entry porch
17 Entry gallery
18 Laundry
19 Dressing room
20 Casbah
21 Spa deck
22 Pool
23 Bedroom
24 Bathroom
25 Common
26 Guest sleeping bay
27 Outdoor guest shower
28 Guest bathroom
29 Outdoor bathtub
30 Outdoor treatment spa/shower
31 Open to below
32 Merlyn's studio
33 Steven's studio

7

8

0   25ft

9

9   View from the west exterior gallery looking towards the master sleeping bay (exterior) and adjacent deck

10   View within the great room looking west to the living area and pool deck beyond

11   Western view from the garden looking beyond the spa deck and pool to the ocean in the near distance

12   Western view from the master sleeping bay looking out towards the Albizia tree forest

PHOTOGRAPHY: DAVID O. MARLOW

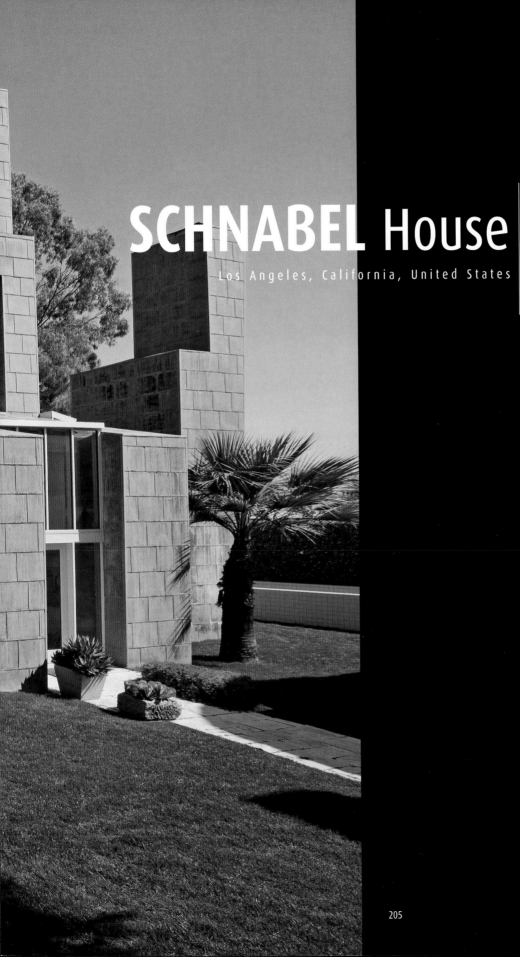

SCHNABEL House

This 530-square-metre (5700-square-foot) house was designed by Frank Gehry as a wedding gift for Ambassador Rockwell Schnabel and his wife Marna, a qualified architect who worked for Gehry Partners previously. Gehry has been quoted as saying that the design was what he had once imagined for his own house.

Completed in 1989, the four-bedroom, five-bathroom home comprises four interconnecting pavilions of glass, wood, stucco and metal (lead and copper). Designed by Nancy Goslee Power & Associates, the landscaped gardens include a lap pool, a reflective pond and an olive grove, providing a tranquil and contemplative outdoor space from which to admire views of the Getty Museum.

The main volume contains a living room, family room, kitchen, dining room, library, media room, study, sauna, three bedrooms (including the master suite) and a plant room across three floors. A breezeway connects a separate

1   The main building, incorporating the living and sleeping areas

2 The exterior of the main building is lead-covered copper

3 First floor plan

4 Basement floor plan

5 View across wading pool

6 View across raised lap pool

7 Master bedroom

PHOTOGRAPHY: NICK SPRINGLETT

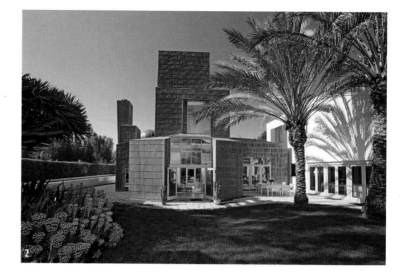

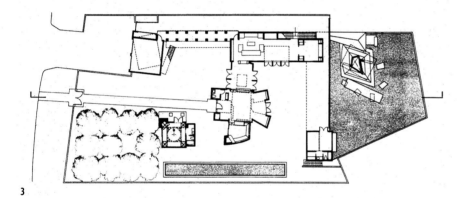

3

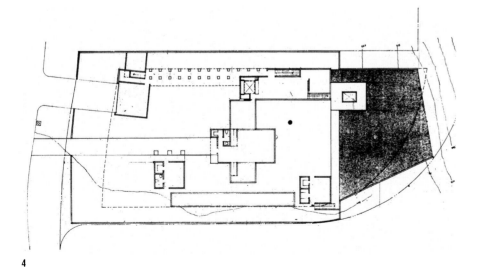

4

pavilion housing the garage and gym to the main building. Two further pavilions include the guest quarters and an office, the latter featuring a visually striking observatory-like dome.

The house was sensitively remodelled and technologically upgraded by the subsequent owner, Jon Platt, an award-winning theatre producer, in close collaboration with Gehry. The update included a comprehensive home-automation system, which includes the activation of a thin film across all bedroom windows to instantaneously mitigate the sun's glare, along with controls for home-security, entertainment, lighting and temperature – all at the tap of a touch screen.

SIERRA Residence

Douglas County, Nevada, United States | ARKIN TILT ARCHITECTS

Situated on the eastern slope of the Sierra Nevada Mountains overlooking the Carson River Valley, this home was carefully designed to take advantage of the rugged beauty of its site. Working with the slope, orientation and dramatic views, the house is structured around a shaded courtyard 'oasis', providing outdoor space protected from both the summer sun and the winter winds. While the garage and guest wing to the west blend into the landscape via living roofs that lift from grade, the main house juts out like a boulder, mimicking the mountains beyond. The south-facing roof of this dominant volume peels up at the corner for passive solar gain and for a dramatic view of snow-capped Job's Peak to the southwest.

Expressive use of alternative construction techniques, solar technologies, salvaged materials and daylight provide texture as well as function for this virtually energy-independent house. Careful shading, high insulation

1   Evening view from the southwest

and thermal mass keep the structures from over-heating in the summer, aided by the flushing of cool night air. Photovoltaic panels on the main roof and trellis generate electricity, and solar thermal panels provide hot water and heating via radiant sand beds under concrete slabs. Natural, efficient and durable materials – straw bale with an earthen finish (using soils found on-site), metal roofing and slatted cement-board siding – are counterpointed by fanciful details – airplane flaps act as sun-shades on the greenhouse and ore-cart wheels support railroad-track trellis beams.

Part buffer from the elements, part viewfinder, the project creates a sustainable mode of living on this challenging site, celebrating its ecology, cultural history and raw beauty.

2   The entrance is flanked by living roofs that peel out of the sagebrush meadow

3   Salvaged airplane flaps provide shade for the integrated greenhouse

4   Adjustable photovoltaic panels shade the protected terrace

5   Solar hot water panels are tucked below the terrace

6

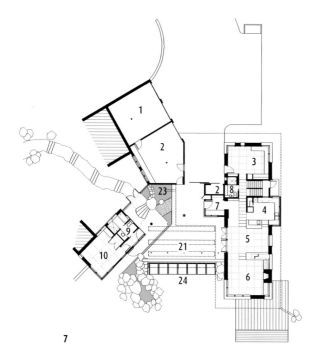

7

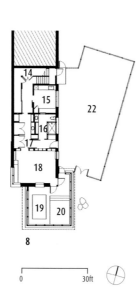

8

1 Garage
2 Storage
3 Office
4 Kitchen
5 Dining
6 Living
7 Entry
8 Powder room
9 Guest bathroom
10 Guest bedroom
11 Bed platform
12 Loft
13 Balcony
14 Mechanical
15 Laundry
16 Master bathroom
17 Master dressing room
18 Master bedroom
19 Pool
20 Greenhouse
21 Terrace with photovoltaic panels above
22 Garden
23 Trombe wall
24 Solar collectors

0   30ft

PHOTOGRAPHY: © WWW.EDWARDCALDWELLPHOTO.COM

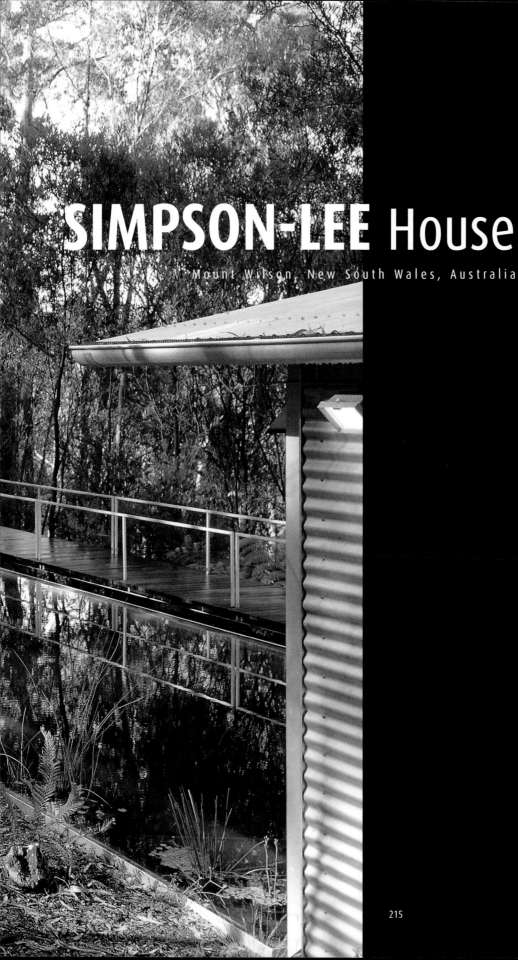

SIMPSON-LEE House

Mount Wilson, New South Wales, Australia

GLENN MURCUTT

Soon after it was built in 1986 on a 3-hectare (7.5-acre) bush lot in the Blue Mountains, the Simpson-Lee House became a benchmark for environmentally responsive and responsible residential architecture. The house was designed by Pritzker Prize-winning architect Glenn Murcutt for a retired intellectual couple – Sheila Simpson-Lee and her husband Geelum, who was formerly dean of the Economics faculty at the University of Sydney. Their brief asked for a private weekend sanctuary with plenty of light. The resulting two-bedroom house with garage and guest quarters won the Wilkinson Award for domestic architecture in 1995 and has since been suggested as a candidate for heritage listing.

Murcutt's career-long ethos of touching the land lightly and making the most of natural conditions for heating and cooling are used to stunning effect in this design. Water is collected from the roof and fed to several tanks for drinking

1   **Pond between the two pavilions collects water for use in the event of bushfire**

215

water and to flush the toilets. A water storage pond located between the two main pavilions services a rooftop sprinkler system in case of bushfire, and the house faces northeast to provide shelter from the harsh west–southwesterly winds.

Open to the vistas of the mountain range beyond, the louvred north façade can be retracted completely, providing an immediate and unhindered connection to the natural beauty outside and allowing the occupants to control light and ventilation. Exterior blinds deflect the harsh summer sun outside the building envelope, stopping the heat before it reaches the main pavilions. The house is thus a working machine with an ongoing relationship with the landscape – a home that can be manipulated directly by its inhabitants to best protect them from the elements.

2 Approach to the house from the driveway

3 The north façade retracted

4 The house sits lightly on the land in its idyllic bush setting

5 The louvred north façade

PHOTOGRAPHY: REINER BLUNCK

1

sky arc

Kentfield, California, United States | **will bruder+PARTNERS**

The crescent plan of this house was derived from the topography and surrounding landscape – the gentle curvature of the Northern California hills. The simple volumes clad in pre-weathered pewter-grey zinc recede into the texture of the local environment.

The house is a choreography of light and shadow, of exterior and interior, and of private and public spaces. Seen from the entry, a framed view of the bay introduces the visitor to the house and its natural surroundings. The sense of movement – past window seats, through doors, across rooms – carries a sensual freshness and continuity throughout the house. The main sitting room expands seamlessly through glass and sliding partitions to a cantilevered wood deck and lawn terrace; boundaries dissolve into the landscape through airy perforated metal railings and translucent fibreglass awnings.

1   West and north façades – looking in towards the living room and bedroom

The dwelling is conceived as an enfolding nest to embrace the family members and their habitation of the house and landscape, adapting with them through the stages of living and coloured by the inherent beauty and wonder of the place.

2   The house in context
3   Façade detail
4   Deck
5   West and north façades – looking in towards the studio

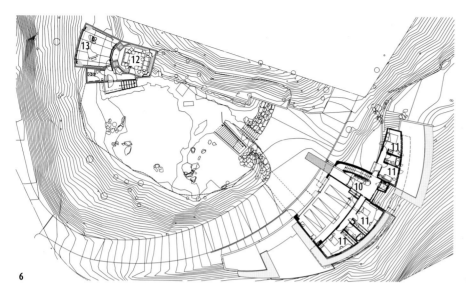

6

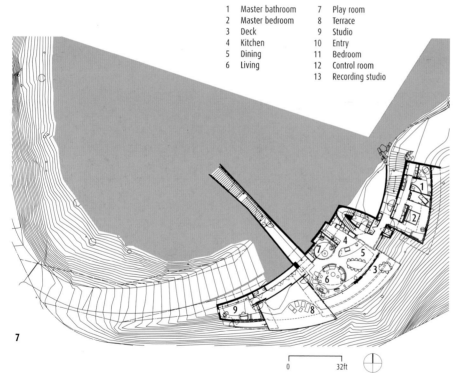

7

1	Master bathroom	7	Play room
2	Master bedroom	8	Terrace
3	Deck	9	Studio
4	Kitchen	10	Entry
5	Dining	11	Bedroom
6	Living	12	Control room
		13	Recording studio

0   32ft

8

6   Entry level plan

7   Main level plan

8   Master bedroom overlook

9   Façade detail

10 Interior dining and exterior deck

11 Living, kitchen and dining

12 Recording studio

PHOTOGRAPHY: BILL TIMMERMAN

1

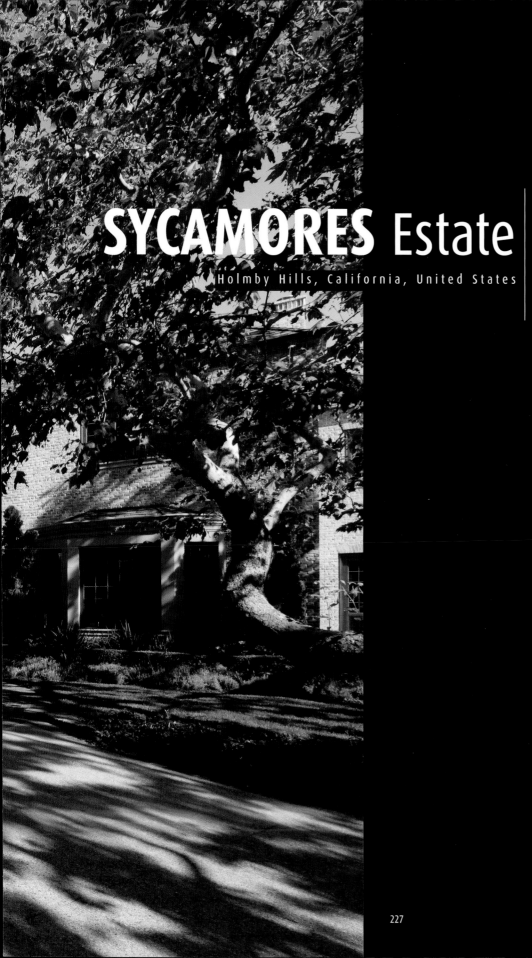

SYCAMORES Estate

Holmby Hills, California, United States

RICHARD MANION ARCHITECTURE

Designed for East Coast clients who wanted the kind of historically inspired house typically found in Westchester County or Connecticut, this estate captures the understated elegance of Harrie T. Lindeberg and the American classicism of John Russell Pope. But the architect was also mindful to design something that would fit into the vernacular of Los Angeles. Rather than predictably covering the façade in mottled tan brick, he selected a handmade brick from Maryland with a natural whitewash finish.

By keeping the exterior motifs formal – a limestone entrance, Doric columns and a big sheltering slate roof – the design honours the owners' affinity for the work of British architect Sir Edwin Lutyens and his oft-collaborator Gertrude Jekyll, the renowned English garden designer. Woodland paths showcase sculptures, a pavilion with stone mosaics, and an outdoor fireplace and seating area.

1   Whitewashed brick handmade in Maryland gives the façade an East Coast feel and subtle strength

The architect also accommodated the owners' love of sports by incorporating a grand back lawn big enough for the father and his three sons to play football. All around the property, English-style gardens designed by Mark Beall take advantage of traditional plantings such as roses, hydrangeas and lavender as well as indigenous succulents and mature sycamores.

In terms of the interiors, the house is accessible and comfortable for the family and their six pets, with no extraneous spaces. This balance is further enhanced by the interior design under the direction of Michael and Alexandra Misczynski of Atelier AM. The eclectic yet restrained interior is elegant with just a hint of the theatrical, mixing Cambodian antiquities with important 1930s pieces.

Yet with all this classicism, the design does not strive for perfect symmetry. Instead, a sense of order was created by allocating the right side of the home to formal gatherings and entertaining, while the left side was designed for family living. Though the entrance hall is a sure statement of Regency style, the home then gently unfolds revealing subtle elements of surprise, such as the sweeping spiral staircase and round gallery spaces that flank either end of the first floor.

2   On the rear façade picturesque wings flank a formal terrace designed for large-scale entertaining as well as casual family fun

3   The outdoor fireplace emulates the style of the house but was rendered in stone to match nearby garden walls

4   Directly outside the family room and breakfast room, with close proximity to the kitchen for service, the family terrace provides a place for outdoor dining and barbecuing

5   The pool house reflects the architecture of the main house and mimics the formal dining room with large arched openings

6   The entry, which is recessed into the house and surrounded by curved walls, was inspired by the work of architect John Russell Pope

7   With a bright cream and green palette, the living room is a curated blend of primitive artefacts and luxe velvets and silks

8   Loro Piana silk drapes and de Gournay wallpaper give the dining room a subtle yet luxurious feeling

9   Picking up the green and cream palette from the living room, the family room is just off the kitchen

10   The master bedroom is edited and minimal, with a 20th-century English tailored feel

11   The guest suite and window bay, which overlooks the pool area, features a circa-1820 Austrian giltwood chandelier and a circa-1800 Georgian mahogany linen press cabinet

12   The breakfast room, with its contemporary leather dining chairs, showcases the leaded windows that can be seen throughout the house

13   Layers of moldings and beams and ovals give the house that authentic period feel, exemplified beautifully in the library with its octagonal coffered ceiling

PHOTOGRAPHY: ERHARD PFEIFFER

TURBULENCE House

Abiquiu, New Mexico, United States | **STEVEN HOLL ARCHITECTS**

Adjacent to adobe courtyard houses built by the artist Richard Tuttle, this small construction is sited atop a windy desert mesa. Its form, imagined like the tip of an iceberg indicating a much larger form below, allows turbulent wind to blow through the centre. The Tuttles' friend Kiki Smith calls it 'a brooch pinned to the mesa'. The house was produced for two locations simultaneously – one for the artist couple in New Mexico and one for an Italian entrepreneur. The interior of each house is finished according to local needs and specificities. The second Turbulence House, made for an exhibition in Vicenza for the Basilica Palladiana, was constructed permanently in a private sculpture park in Schio, Italy.

The architects worked with A. Zahner and Co, a Kansas City sheet metal fabrication company that utilises digital definition combined with craftsmanship to produce highly intricate metal shapes and forms. By means of parametric logic, solid materials can be converted into engineered

1   View at mesa entrance road

233

assemblies to an accuracy once considered impossible. The majority of the construction documents were generated electronically using three-dimensional computer design.

The stressed skin and aluminum rib construction was digitally prefabricated in Kansas City and bolted together on site. The sizes of the panels are governed by the inside dimensions of a generic 12-metre (40-foot) shipping container, thus the panels are limited to a 2.5-metre-wide (8-foot) module. A total of 30 metal panels, each with a unique shape, are fabricated to form the entire 'shell' of the house.

Computer generated templates were created to ensure the absolute minimum amount of aluminium was wasted in the production of the exterior panels. The smallest is 1.8 by 3 metres (6 by 10 feet) and the largest is 2.5 by 7 metres (8 by 23 feet) – and the average unit weight for the aluminium panels is 3.5 kilograms (8 pounds).

The majority of the window openings are north-facing to minimise direct heat gain, and small relative to the total surface area of the house, allowing for minimal heat gain during the day. The two slotted window-skylights located at the northern and southern top edge of the house allow for heated air from inside to escape.

2   View at mesa entrance road after snow
3   Second floor plan
4   First floor plan
5   Kitchen prefabricated in Austin, Texas
6   View to east horizon, with furniture by Richard Tuttle

PHOTOGRAPHY: PAUL WARCHOL

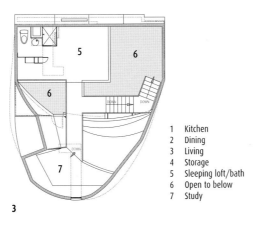

1 Kitchen
2 Dining
3 Living
4 Storage
5 Sleeping loft/bath
6 Open to below
7 Study

3

4

0   10ft

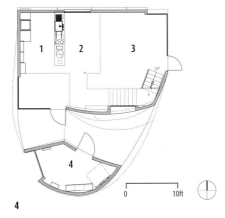

VILLA in Lyngby

Lyngby, Denmark | **HENNING LARSEN ARCHITECTS**

Situated on a sloping plot, this 190-square-metre (2000-square-foot) villa enjoys expansive views of a large garden featuring charming old trees and a small lake. The villa was constructed primarily with Nordic materials, which creates a fine connection between the existing architecture of the area and the clear, simple design of the house.

The double-storey villa features two extensions to the ground floor – one of which constitutes the entrance hall and the other the kitchen. Above the two extensions, small terraces facing east and west make it possible to enjoy the sun throughout the day. The terraces are accessible from the first floor.

To the south and north, the façades are fitted with large double-height windows, providing all rooms in the house with ample daylight and an attractive, open dining room.

1–3   View from the garden
4   Balcony with built-in seating

5   Second floor plan

6   First floor plan

7   Kitchen

8   View of living area from lounge

9   View of living area from dining

PHOTOGRAPHY: ADAM MØRK (1–4, 7–9); HENNING LARSEN ARCHITECTS (5, 6)

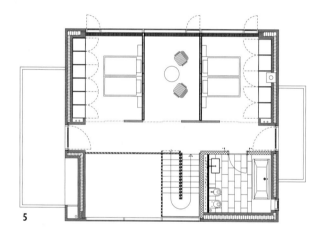

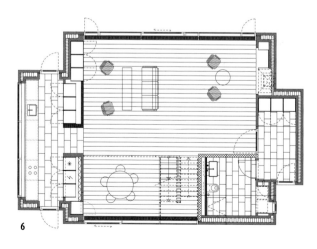

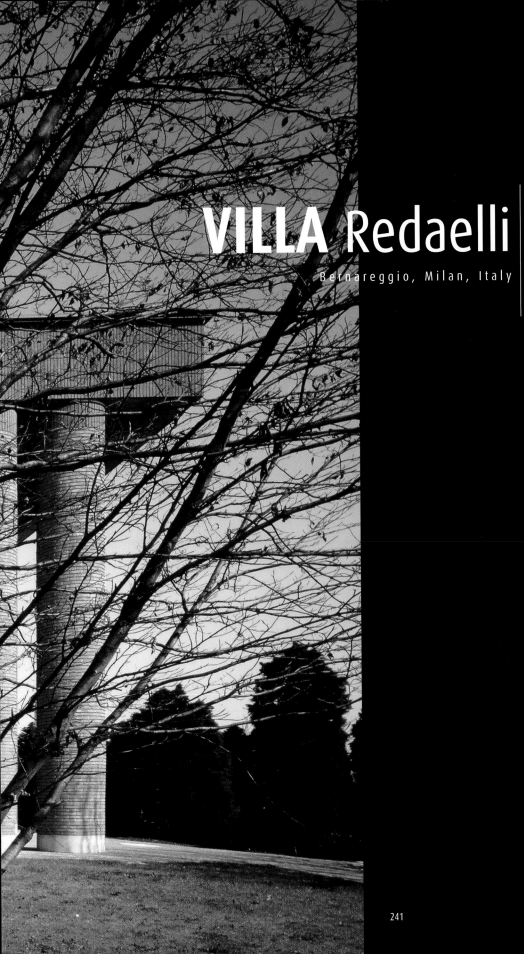

VILLA Redaelli

Bernareggio, Milan, Italy | **MARIO BOTTA**

The 2500-square-metre (27,000-square-foot) villa is located in a residential area north of the town of Bernareggio, in the province of Milan, in a typical suburban setting with single-family houses. The villa rises to a height of three storeys.

On the first floor, in addition to the entrance, the entire space is completely open to the garden and features an indoor swimming pool and connected utilities. The large living room, the kitchen and the master bedroom are on the second floor; the library, two other bedrooms and bathrooms are located on the third floor.

The east façade of the house, set parallel to the street, has a massive appearance with double walls faced with terracotta bricks, designed for noise protection. This façade features external stairs connecting the garden with the library on the third floor.

1   View of southwest façade

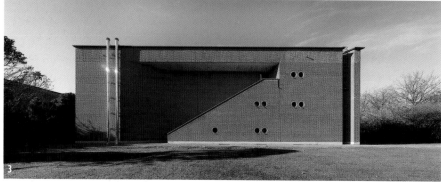

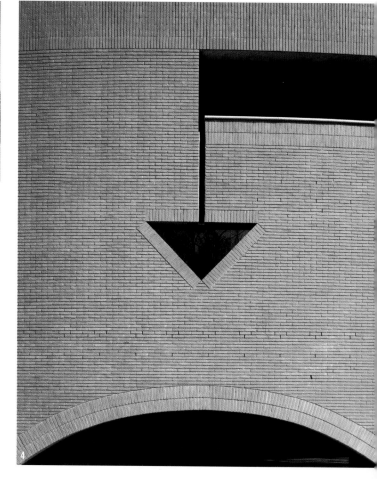

2 Front view of the west façade

3 View of the east façade

4 Detail of the effect created by the openings on the west façade

5 View of the outdoor staircase on the east façade

6 Night view of the west façade

The convex west façade, which faces the garden, curves to form an arc that ends at the northern tip. It is a particularly complex façade, with recessed areas in relation to the eaves, thus creating a broad portico on three floors and deep loggias on the third storey.

Two massive binate columns mark the southwest corner of the entrance and create an indoor–outdoor transition area between the rooms in the villa and the park. The use of terracotta brickwork for the entire exterior masonry lends a sense of unity to the architectural form, which is embellished with windows and openings in different shapes including arches, arrows and rectangles.

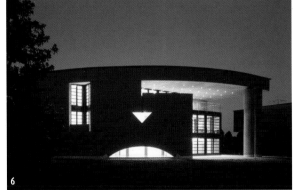

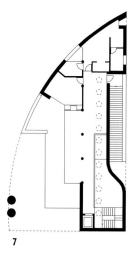

7

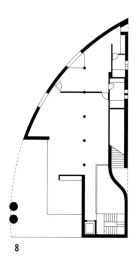

8

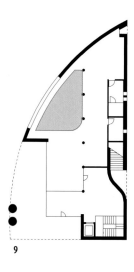

9

10

11

12

7	Third floor plan
8	Second floor plan
9	First floor plan
10&15	View of the second floor characterised by the full-length window
11	Swimming pool on the second floor; the arched window overlooks the garden
12	Living room on the second floor
13	Overall interior view of the second and first floor
14	Covered terrace on the second floor

PHOTOGRAPHY: PINO MUSI (1, 4, 6, 10, 12, 14, 15); ENRICO CANO (2, 3, 5, 11, 13)

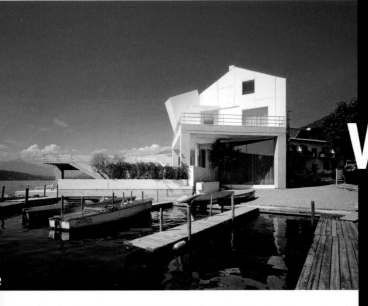

VILLA S

Millstatt, Austria

COOP HIMMELB(L)AU

This vacation home lies on the shore of a lake at the southernmost tip of Millstatt, a health resort in Carinthia, Austria. The summer villa was realised as a renovation project, as building regulations required that the contours of the previous structure and the angle of its roof be preserved. As a result of these specifications, the vacation home's form is defined by the original gable roof, a slanted tower, a generously defined exterior, and an inimitable spatial structure. The simple structural concrete, white painted surfaces of wood and metal, and consciously anti-tectonic joint pattern lend the home a sense of ease and serenity.

A 'table' platform of reinforced concrete elevates the upper area of the former house so that a free floor plan is possible on the first level. The 'table' separates the private rooms in the upper area from the semi-public, transparent rooms in the lower area.

1   View from the south towards the villa with the 'table' that serves as a terrace and carries the upper part of the villa

2   View from the east (neighbour's view) before the pavilion was added

3   The concrete walkway, stair tower and 'table' with living room below and private rooms above

247

4   Second floor view
5   Living room / terrace
6   Second floor
7   Third floor stair tower
8   Stair tower / view from the third floor into the stair tower
9   Kitchen and docks

A terrace extends the living room on the second floor out toward the lake. The room, with its ceiling-high glass panels, can be opened, allowing inside and outside spaces to flow together. The house is also transparent on the street side, another of its important characteristics. Here, local artists have the opportunity to use the public area as an exhibition space.

Directly above the docks – where boats can be hoisted up by means of a cable winch – lies a kitchen counter. When the window is open, it is almost as though the motorboat hangs directly in the kitchen. Sicilian olive trees adorn the interior and exterior spaces, adding a Mediterranean touch.

From the terrace, a concrete stairway leads to a cedar-wood pavilion that juts out over the lake on an elevated walkway. On the underside of this concrete platform is a swing for gliding over Lake Millstatt. From the elevated walkway, one arrives across a concrete walkway into the living room gallery and the television room. A slanting tower-house is set atop the gallery to expand the private accommodations on the upper level.

On the lower floor are business, storage and technical spaces, along with a mahogany-panelled wine cellar complete with a bar and ample seating for tastings. The wine rack with irregular cylindrical recesses, also designed by the architect, can ascend from the cellar into the living area when needed.

8

9

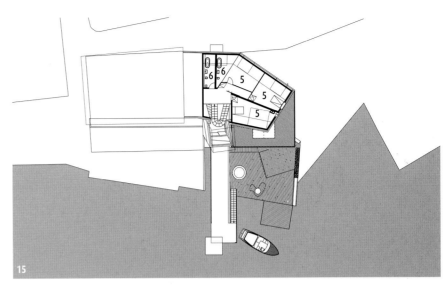

15

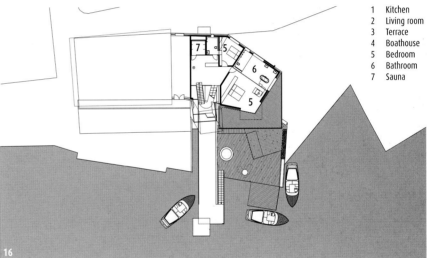

1	Kitchen
2	Living room
3	Terrace
4	Boathouse
5	Bedroom
6	Bathroom
7	Sauna

16

10 Living room on first floor with glass doors closed and curtains drawn

11 Wine rack elevated for use in living room

12 Bar for wine tastings; at the rear is the door to the wine cellar

13 Wine rack elevated for use in living room

14 Master bedroom with open bathroom

15 Third floor plan

16 Second floor plan

17 First floor plan

PHOTOGRAPHY: © GERALD ZUGMANN; PLANS: © COOP HIMMELB(L)AU

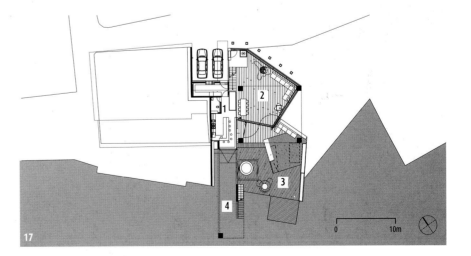

0   10m

17

VILLA Veneto

Sydney, New South Wales, Australia | MICHAEL SUTTOR

The client brief for this project was to design a landmark residence to suit a large waterfront property with iconic views across Sydney Harbour to the Harbour Bridge and Opera House. Fortunately, the unrestricted budget enabled the design to address the many challenges presented by the site without compromise.

While the views to the northwest are spectacular, the afternoon sun reflects strongly from the harbour. To create access to the site, which falls steeply from the roadway, garaging was provided at the street level. A generous high-speed lift was designed to take passengers down to a two-storey cloistered gallery, which surrounds an internal courtyard and contains the front door of the house. The major rooms open onto this courtyard, which links all parts of the house. Sheltered loggias facing the harbour deflect the glare, with the stairs positioned on the side to allow entry to the waterfront without disrupting the view.

1   A stone stair leads to the waterfront

A timelessly elegant design is achieved through well-proportioned classical detailing, giving this significant villa an imposing but not dominating presence on the foreshore of Sydney Harbour.

Michael Suttor

2   The building terracing to the waterfront

3   Wrought-iron entry gate at the front door

4   View across the loggia

5   The entry courtyard leads to the front door

6   A shuttered loggia shelters the rooms behind

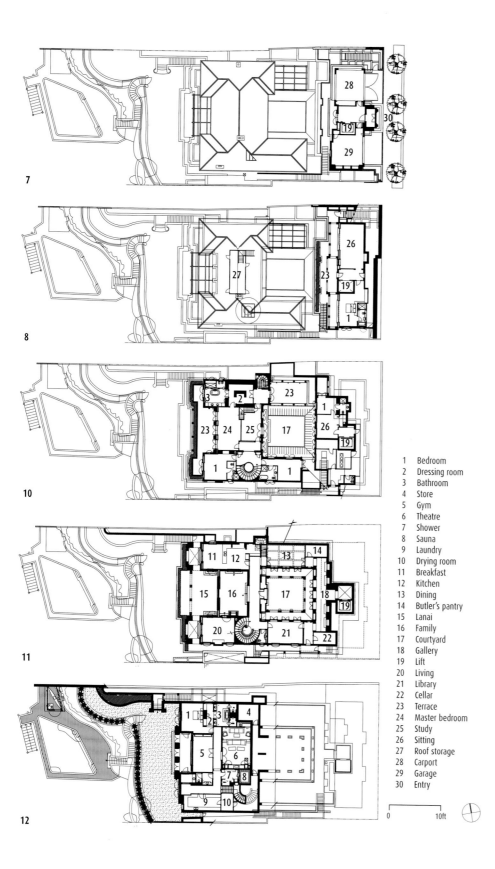

1 Bedroom
2 Dressing room
3 Bathroom
4 Store
5 Gym
6 Theatre
7 Shower
8 Sauna
9 Laundry
10 Drying room
11 Breakfast
12 Kitchen
13 Dining
14 Butler's pantry
15 Lanai
16 Family
17 Courtyard
18 Gallery
19 Lift
20 Living
21 Library
22 Cellar
23 Terrace
24 Master bedroom
25 Study
26 Sitting
27 Roof storage
28 Carport
29 Garage
30 Entry

0   10ft

PHOTOGRAPHY: LUCA VILLATA

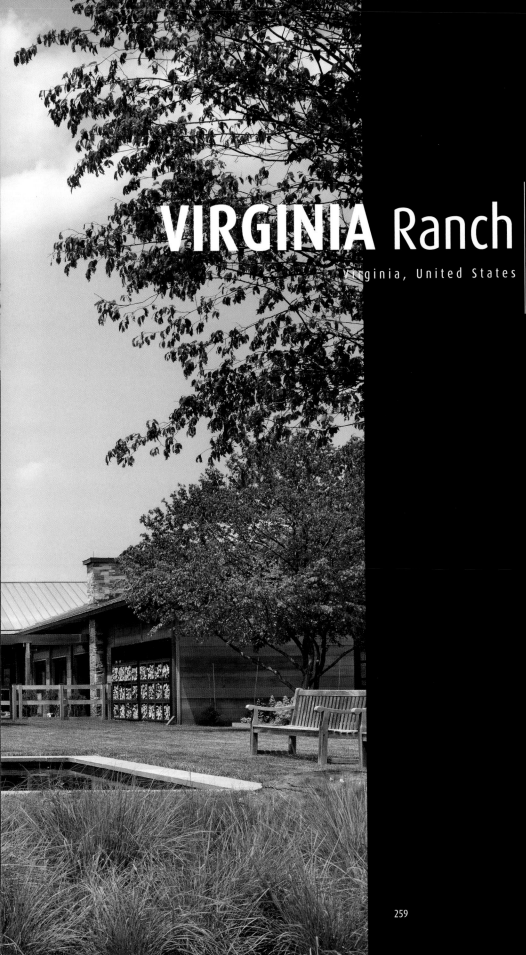

VIRGINIA Ranch

Virginia, United States

DIAMOND SCHMITT ARCHITECTS

The Virginia Ranch is located in the eastern foothills of the Blue Ridge Mountains, a part of the State of Virginia known for large horse estates and traditional architecture. The 220-hectare (550-acre) site encompasses a series of rolling hills, with numerous stands of mature black oak and several creeks cut through the property, one of which has been transformed to create a small pond and wetland.
The clients expressed a strong desire for a house that was unlike others in the surrounding area, a house that would enhance their appreciation of this unique landscape. As owners of several horses, a key component of the project was an eight-stall horse barn.

The house is arranged around an intimate, landscaped entry courtyard and the horse barn forms one side of this space. Approaching the home over the site's landscape of rolling hills, the barn is the first element that comes into view. It begins an entry sequence that takes the visitor under a covered walkway, slipping between carport and

1   View of house from the north

259

barn, and leading along one edge of the garden courtyard to the entrance of the house itself.

The house is sited so as to maintain complete privacy from the road while enjoying magnificent views of the forests, the new pond and the Blue Ridge Mountains to the south and the west. The ground floor is arranged around the four sides of this courtyard. A double-height living and dining space with adjacent kitchen, pantry and a three-season screened porch open to the southern mountain views. A master bedroom wing with a library looks west, with direct views to the paddocks. The second floor provides guest rooms accessed from their own stair at the entry while a home-office and exercise room are located above the master bedroom suite. The double-height living and dining space has 10 sets of French doors and four large-scale lift-and-slide mahogany doors that open to connect the garden courtyard to a covered porch. Heating and cooling is provided by a geothermal system and, in order to open the house to the outdoors whenever possible, all rooms are provided with operable windows and fans for airflow.

2   View of house from the south

3   Inner courtyard

4   View through living room to courtyard

5   View of master bedroom wing from courtyard

PHOTOGRAPHY: TOM ARBAN

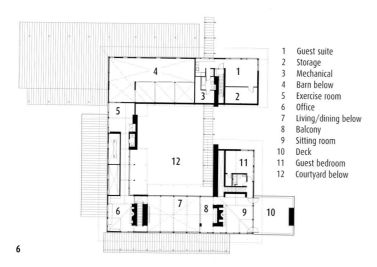

1   Guest suite
2   Storage
3   Mechanical
4   Barn below
5   Exercise room
6   Office
7   Living/dining below
8   Balcony
9   Sitting room
10 Deck
11 Guest bedroom
12 Courtyard below

6

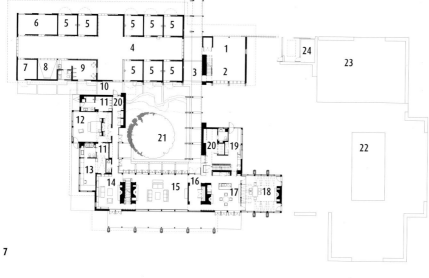

1   Carport
2   Firewood storage
3   Entry
4   Barn aisle
5   Stall
6   Feed storage
7   Equipment storage
8   Wash stall
9   Tack room
10 Breezeway
11 Dressing room
12 Master bedroom
13 Office
14 Library
15 Living/dining
16 Entrance
17 Kitchen
18 Screened porch
19 Pantry
20 Mudroom
21 Courtyard
22 Pool
23 Boules court
24 Pool mechanical room

7

INDEX of Architects